A Prodigal's Journey Home

By Robert Grant

Acknowledgements

There are many who have contributed to this work both knowingly and unknowingly. First, I would begin with my own Father, Hoke Loyd Grant, who delighted in me as the first child of his old age (after a five-year gap, there would follow 4 more). He loved me and showed me what it felt like to be a beloved son. Second, Lloyd James Moore, my step-father, and when I finally grew up, my Dad. He showed me how a father loves without expecting or receiving love in return. Pastor Howard K. Ryan, a father in the faith who saw in the wreck of my life a calling as a minister of the Gospel. He guided and encouraged me in learning to walk that walk. The numerous other spiritual men who spoke into my life and helped me fulfill a measure of that calling. To the Promise Keepers' group and many men's authors whose writing encouraged and challenged me to live out my faith. To these and to other men, living or ascended, who contributed to my continuing development as a man, I say thank you. To my wife Cheri, who proofreads and offers great insight into the compiling of this work, thank you my love. To missionary and author Debby Davis, who serves as my editor and assists with publishing, thank you. And finally, to the ultimate Father, God the Father Almighty who gives me the very breath I breathe and from whose Words the premise of this book is drawn. He never abandoned me in my wandering and called me His own upon my return. My eternal gratitude is owed and given to Him.

Preface

In my life I have lived in all four corners of the continental United States. Traveled as far east as Scotland, as far west as Japan. North to the Arctic Circle and south to Guam. I have lived at home with family, in barracks, on ships, in apartments, house trailers, homes. Bought and sold real estate and been a landlord. Been single, married, divorced, remarried, widowed, and remarried. Raised and buried children and grandchildren. Experienced the full life spectrum from triumphant joy to heart wrenching tragedy. Served in the Navy on submarines and surface ships. Been a worker bee, manager, entrepreneur, pastor, author and speaker. The last two are where I am now. So what, you may say! Why should I care?

My point is, I have lived a lot, seen a lot, endured a lot, and I have discovered this truth. We are all on a journey to the day when we will meet God, our Creator face to face! On that day, in my opinion, we will have to answer maybe two questions. First, what did you decide concerning My Son Jesus the Christ? If the answer is something like, "I chose not to follow Him and took my own path." Then our interview is over and we head into the unimaginable horror of an eternity separated from God. If the answer is, "I chose to accept Him as my Lord and Savior and I claim status as a son because of His work." Then we will be approved to enter eternity in the presence of God, made whole and new. I also believe we will be asked a followup question. "What did you do to further the Kingdom of Heaven during your life?" It is in the answer to this question where we will discover what of our life is treasure to be enjoyed for eternity and what is hay and stubble to be consumed by fire. It is this impending meeting for us all that prompts this writing.

As one who has contributed more than his fair share of hay and stubble to the great bonfire scheduled for the end of time, I hope by sharing my experience and discovery to assist others in avoiding some of the traps that I found. I would tell the reader that you are never too far gone to turn towards God and begin to follow His leading. There is no act too disgusting, no failure so catastrophic, no event so tragic as to cause Him to reject you, if you approach Him in the right way. To that end, I hope to demonstrate that we all miss the mark. We all have to turn away from our choices and discover His choices for us. He provides many to help us along the way. The great thing is others are recovering from the same things we are. They struggle in the same way we do. They suffer fear and doubt, act out of emotion instead of relationship and all the other issues we men have. Yet, the Father communicates this. "Come as you are, walk with My Son Jesus, and be changed by the journey." Turn the page, brother. Find out where you are in your life journey. Hook up with your brothers and be changed and ready to meet Him on your day!

Table of Contents

Chapter 1: We Are All Prodigals   10

Chapter 2: My Prodigal Journey   20

Chapter 3: From the Pigpen to the Salt Mine   32

Chapter 4: A Beloved Son Well Pleasing to the Father   42

Chapter 5: The Bonds of Brotherhood   54

Chapter 6: Benevolent Fathers   74

Chapter 7: The Journey Continues   90

Appendix A: Finding Our Big Brother   100

Appendix B: Telling Your Story   104

We Are All Prodigals

It seems that if you have attended a church for any period of your life, you have heard the story of the Prodigal Son. And the typical teaching of the lesson sounds like this: this worthless son took his inheritance and wasted it, came home and begged, so the Father took him back. Don't be a prodigal, come to the altar and repent. Did you ever consider that maybe, just maybe, the story was not a story of condemnation, not about judgment, not about the wasteful son, or his brother, the diligent, unforgiving son, but instead it is a story of the Father's love for humanity and His boundless desire for restoration with us. Let's look together.

Luke 15:11-32, And he said, "There was a man who had two sons. (12) And the younger of them said to his father, 'Father, give me the share of property that is coming to me.' And he divided his property between them. (13) Not many days later, the younger son gathered all he had and took a journey into a far country, and there he squandered his property in reckless living. (14) And when he had spent everything, a severe famine arose in that country, and he began to be in need. (15) So he went and hired himself out to one of the citizens of that country, who sent him into his fields to feed pigs. (16) And he was longing to be fed with the pods that the pigs ate, and no one gave him anything. (17) "But when he came to himself, he said, 'How many of my father's hired servants have more than enough bread, but I perish here with hunger! (18) I will arise and go to my father, and I will say to him, "Father, I have sinned against heaven and before you. (19) I am no longer worthy to be called your son. Treat me as one of your hired servants."' (20) And he arose and came to his father. But while he was still a long way off, his father saw him and felt compassion, and ran and embraced him and kissed him. (21) And the son said to him, 'Father, I have sinned against heaven and before you. I am no longer worthy to be called your son.' (22) But the father said to his servants, 'Bring quickly the best robe, and put it on him, and put a ring on his hand, and shoes on his feet. (23) And bring the fattened calf and kill it, and let us eat and celebrate. (24) For this my son was dead, and is alive again; he was lost, and is found.' And they began to celebrate. (25) "Now his older son was in the field, and as he came and drew near to the house, he heard music and dancing. (26) And he called one of the servants and asked what these things meant. (27) And he said to him, 'Your brother has come, and your father has killed the fattened calf, because he has received him back safe and sound.' (28) But he was angry and refused to go in. His father came out and entreated him, (29) but he answered his father, 'Look, these many years I have served you, and I never disobeyed your command, yet you never gave me a young goat, that I might celebrate with my friends. (30) But when this son of yours came, who has devoured your property with prostitutes, you killed the fattened calf for him!' (31) And he said to him, 'Son, you are always with me, and all that is mine is yours. (32) It was fitting to celebrate and be glad, for this your brother was dead, and is alive; he was lost, and is found.'

The first thing I notice, is the word prodigal does not appear here anywhere. In fact, if you search the Greek, you will not find it there either. The word is added as a page break by editors to make the story easier to locate. Second, it tells the story of three characters, not one. The two sons and the father. In point of fact, two prodigals and a father. It begins with the younger son chafing at authority and asking to inherit and be set free. The father's response? He gave both sons their inheritance. One set out to be free of all responsibility, the other set about trying to prove he was worthy of the inheritance that was given. In the end, we find both had wasted their inheritance. The younger son chose life with the world, the older, a life of good works and discipline (religion). Both will rob us of our true inheritance, the loving, living relationship that comes from knowing God the Father. Last, it is narrated by a third unmentioned son. Jesus, the Son revealing the heart of God, His Father. Let us look at these in detail.

The younger son took all he had to the world. The world embraced him. There was always something else to buy, some new thing to eat or drink, some new and often forbidden experience to embrace. Many times the preacher will encourage us to avoid the drunkenness and sexual sins of the "prodigal," but scripture only says riotous living, specific sins are not mentioned (although the older brother accuses him of going with prostitutes). Life was a riot, a protest against the status quo established by the Father. For us today it can mean buying things on credit, eating out instead of cooking at home, having three TVs or the newest smartphone. Some of these things are not evil by themselves, but the mindless pursuit, the lust for possessions is the problem. Or maybe we are grasping for power and position, throwing others under the bus to advance our own cause. Promotion when earned is a good thing, but careers that consume our lives or compromise our character are riotous living. Of course, it can mean sexual sin, drunkenness and perversion, gambling, fornication and such like. These things are a trap of the enemy, Satan. The world, and the spirit that is in and of the world promise freedom and pleasure that only a relationship with God can provide. The end of all worldly pleasures is death. We become dead to our conscience, dead to feelings, dead to relationships, and if we do not turn, eventually we will be dead to God Himself.

"When he came to himself…" All the behaviors listed above have an ending point. Lust, power, and possessions will leave us empty and friendless in the end. When the younger son realized the futility of his path, he turned around (repented) and he got this revelation. The Father's plan, as evidenced by the servants' lives, was "enough and some extra." Enough work, enough recognition, enough rejoicing and celebrating with friends and enough to share. These things are not prohibited, they are balanced and to be experienced in abundance. *John 10:10 "The thief comes only to steal and kill and destroy. I came that they may have life and have it abundantly."* (emphasis mine) This is the plan, and it only succeeds in the Father's house (don't read this as church house, that is another subject). The Father's house is the place where He lives and orchestrates the lives of His children for their good. That is the place we must get back to. The disobedient son recognized this truth and turned home. We will leave him to his journey at this point and look at his brother.

There is the religious son, I don't call him obedient, because he missed the lessons of the father in much the same way the younger did. While the younger took freedom to the extreme, the older took on the bondage of proving himself worthy. He observed the younger brother and said in his heart, "that is wasteful, disrespectful, hurtful, I will never do that. To guard against that, I will labor to show how worthy and respectful and honorable I am." There are two failures here, the first being that he judges his brother and eventually develops a hatred for him. Second, at the beginning, the father gave the full inheritance to both sons. This son never accepted that and just continued to labor. He never took advantage of the freedom or the promises of the father's provision, he just labored. Labor without relationship leads to bitterness and judgement. While his assessment of his brother's actions was accurate, and his desire to avoid that behavior commendable; his bitterness and judgement of his brother and his father was wrong. He got the truth of discipline, but missed the revelation of freedom. We must understand that we should avoid sin, but we will never completely achieve a sinless life in this body. No service, study, or self-denial will get us the righteousness that is only achieved by a loving relationship with the Father which is paid for by faith in the work of Jesus the Christ. 1 Corinthians 13:3 "If I give away all I have, and if I deliver up my body to be burned, but have not love, I gain nothing." Diligence and obedience without love, like greed and debauchery, still lead to death.

Now to the father. The father is portrayed first of all, as generous. What he did for his younger son, giving the inheritance, he did for the other as well. Next he is patient. He does not seek to bring correction into the life of either son until that son approaches. The father is observant. When the son was a long way off, he saw him, and ran to his son. He did not even hear the confession of the son's repentance before taking action. He covered the evidence of his sin with the "Best Robe." He restored his sonship with a ring, the symbol of the father's authority. He gave him a new standing with new shoes. And, most importantly, He restored him to fellowship in the family with a feast. This repentant son entered the father's house in a relationship and with standing despite his past failures. God our Father, like the two son's father will let us plunge into the depths of depravity, or labor in the futility of self righteousness until we, like the younger son, get sick of our own way. He does not desire this for us, but He gives us the free choice of working it out for ourselves. We are never out of sight of the Father. He sees us in all our weakness and struggle, but often He waits for us because He knows that we can only be delivered when we come to Him in repentance. He is eager to restore us.

The older son, despite being diligent, despite possessing freely all the father had, despite the father's constant presence, was unable to see beyond the younger son's failures. His knowledge of the facts blinded him to the truth of the Father's love, grace and generosity, not only to his brother, but to him as well. All he could have wanted, he needed only ask, but instead he labored, and judged, and hated, and the story would have us believe that he remained outside of the celebration of relationship with the father.

In the same manner, God the Father has provided an inheritance for all people through Jesus the Christ. Belief in His death, burial, resurrection and ascension, coupled with the confession of that belief, restore us to being children of God. Notice these things about the story. The depth of our sin, no matter how egregious, no matter how long, no matter what it is, does not keep us from restoration if we come to the end of ourselves, repent, and return to the Father. He will restore us to the position of Adam at creation, that of being a created son of God. Notice also that no labor, no matter how professional and disciplined, will earn us entry to the house. See also that holding another's sin against them will also keep us from fellowship. If I am offended by another person because of their sin, I cannot have fellowship with the Father. I, like the first son, must repent as well to be welcomed in. If I repent, He will run to me, cover me, restore me, give me standing, and bring me into His fellowship, His house to live forever.

Now, why is this so important? I would refer you to the title, "A Prodigal's Journey Home." In my own life I have wandered from the pig-pen to the labor of the Father's fields and back again numerous times without ever coming to the Father's House. Not only that, as a minister, I have observed that in the lives of others as well. We become disgusted with our sin, and promise to do better, so we quit drinking, smoking, chasing after things of the flesh and purpose to do good. So we serve on committees and volunteer and give in the offering, but never get the truth of relationship because we know our sin and we feel that we are not worthy of relationship. Eventually the serving without relationship wears us out because we are not getting anywhere in our own righteousness so we quit, or worse, we return to the pigpen. The enemy will keep us going back and forth like a ping-pong ball if we let him. It is only in turning to the Father, learning who He says we are, accepting that to be true and then walking it out as He leads that brings us to His House. It is a journey, not a destination. Some years ago, I learned this truth. God is calling out to us through Jesus. His call sounds something like this. "Come as you are, walk with Me, be changed on the journey!" It is that truth that I want you to see. All of this life is a journey to enter the next life. We are continually being transformed by the leading of His Spirit. We are to accept this calling, encourage others in theirs, and walk with Him daily.

In the chapters that follow, I hope to encourage you with stories from my own journey. And the discovery of four significant truths in the journey home. Those truths are: I am a beloved son of God, no matter what. I am to be bonded to brothers on the journey. I need them and they need me. The Father is benevolent to all who come to Him, and we are to emulate that in our lives. Finally, it is a journey, not a destination. I never arrive until I cross over into eternity.

Questions for Reflection.

1. Where are you on your journey? In the pigpen? On the road home? In the fields? Entered into the Father's house? We will all be in one of these places. Consider carefully where you are, and take steps to enter into or remain in the Father's house.

2. If you are in the pigpen, what do you need to do?

3. If you are in the field, what do you need to do?

4. If you have entered the Father's House. How do you stay there?

Each of these questions focuses on a responsive action. He is calling us to repentance. Our response is to repent. He is calling us to cease fruitless labor and enter labor that is in response to His love for us. He is calling us to not judge our fellow believers, or even unbelievers, because in reality, we do not know the struggle of their journey or the power of His deliverance in their lives. Next, we respond to having entered the Father's House, by rejecting the voice of the enemy, who says our sin is too great. We also reject that same voice that demands we work to earn that which is freely given. We embrace the freedom the Father provides and respond to that freedom by laboring to help others along on their journey. If my labor does not help me or someone else get closer to the Father, it is not the Father's choice of labor for me. Finally, the secret of the location of the Father's house - it is in my own beating heart. There He takes His residence with Jesus the Son, and the Holy Spirit. Communion with them in my innermost thoughts, through song, and scripture and fellowship, protects me and keeps me on my Journey until I arrive at His final destination for me.

Chapter Two

My Prodigal Journey

1 Corinthians 13:11, When I was a child, I spoke like a child, I thought like a child, I reasoned like a child. When I became a man, I gave up childish ways.

Prodigal - (N) One who spends money or resources freely or recklessly; wastefully extravagant.

I wasn't always a prodigal. I was born in January 1953 in a fairly typical American household. My father was a career Naval veteran of WWII and my mother, the daughter of a sharecropper. Dad was 46 at my birth and I was the apple of his eye. He had already finished a thirty year Navy career, having lied about his age to enter service. He had worked his way up from the enlisted to the officer ranks based on merit (a pattern I would follow some 22 years later). Having been around the world and done everything, all he wanted was to have a wife and family and never leave home again. He accomplished that. My earliest memory of Dad is him taking me everywhere he went and proclaiming that I was "the best little buddy he ever had." For fourteen years he taught me to work hard, to study and achieve by force of will and working within the boundaries of the system. His home instruction helped me skip a grade in elementary school, which would mark me emotionally later in life. He had many sayings, among them were, "Always do the right thing." and "Never start a fight, but if you must fight, finish it." That last one led to my first trouble in school. I was in the first grade and a fellow student named Carl had some very thick glasses because corrective surgery for crossed eyes was either not yet a thing or was financially prohibitive, I don't know which. Many of the boys were chanting about "cross-eyed Carl" and for some reason it inflamed my sense of righteousness. I picked one of the boys and had to be pulled off of him. My mother's response, "What is wrong with you teachers that you would allow that to happen?" My Father? "Good job son, look out for the weak." Carl's mother? Well, she called to thank my parents for raising such a good and responsible son. And there the first seeds of being a prodigal were planted. I embraced the idea that I could correct what was wrong in the world with my fists, if it was a righteous cause. During this season, I learned to work and earn (no allowance in our household, you earned or did not have), received praise for success and discipline for infractions (read spanking). I played ball, learned to swim, fish and camp, joined the Boy Scouts. In other words, I was living the child's American dream. I also started attending the Baptist Church around the corner and became saved. Dad never talked with me about faith, and he did not attend church because of the "hypocrites located therein." And then, August 20, 1967, something happened. I had been camping a couple of days before and came home with Strep Throat. I was in bed and ill, and my mother woke me to say Dad was sick and she was taking him to the hospital.

Before daylight that morning, he was gone, and I was now what He had prepared me to be "The Man of The House." Too early, unprepared, my childhood cut short, I now was babysitter to four younger siblings ages 5 to 9. It would begin a life of caring for others that continues to this day, and I thought, "I have become a man." I was wrong!

Two years would pass. We would build a new house from Dad's life insurance. Mom had been a nurse and continued to work, because the widows' benefit and social security were woefully inadequate. We were poor, but I never knew it. There were clothes, food, Christmas presents and such. So while we didn't have excess, we had enough. We even went on our first family vacation. I had adjusted to my new role. No, after school sports or clubs for me, just get home and take care of the "kids." To be fair, I had the weekend to spend time with my friends, but scouts and other activities except church faded away. Mom and my brothers and sisters started coming to church as a family, which I thought was a good thing. I was angry at God, though. He had taken my dad away. It was years before I understood more of the truth in that arena. While we missed Dad, things were, mostly, good.

Then a change came. My mother was still a young woman and started to attend some adult dance parties for singles and even dated a little bit. One day, after talking to us in advance, she brought home a man she was dating. We would see him several times over the next few months as they courted. Loyd Moore was to be her new husband and our step-father. My siblings were excited. They met him in the car when he pulled up shouting "you're going to be our new daddy." My internal fangs were bared and I may have actually growled. "Not mine," I said to myself. Who was this stranger who thought he could take my Dad's place? The little kids needed a dad, okay. Mom needed a husband. Okay, but not me. I was the man of this house at 16 and he would find that out. While the others called him Daddy, I called him Lloyd. It was a rebellion of the highest order, and another seed of the prodigal life was planted.

Loyd was a good man, and a Godly one. He bore my insolence with grace and gave me love in return. Still wounded and angry, I largely rejected his love unless I needed something. He gave without asking in return, provided wisdom and counsel, loaned me money he did not have to loan and many other things. Looking back, he was the first man (and one of a very few) to truly show me the heart of God the Father in human form. His love and kindness to my mother and her children slowly won me over. I remember taking a stand in his defense to my siblings before he ever became "Dad" to me. And "Dad" he became. His character and love won me over. He loved God intently, and the Jesus pattern of life was evident in his living. Even to his last years as he suffered the ravages of emphysema, the once strong construction superintendent was bound to a wheelchair and his strength gone. We would sit together drinking coffee and talking of scripture and Jesus' love for us. I officiated at his memorial service in 2006 and was struck by the hundreds in attendance. This man, with an eighth-grade education, had impacted so many with his life. At this writing, I know I have too, but not always in the manner he did. Often, my impact was that of a prodigal.

I graduated high school at seventeen and entered my freshman year of college about three weeks later. I was eager to be on my own, but in reality I was emotionally just a child. I lacked the discipline to apply myself to the study required, was arrogant with my instructors, and after about eighteen months the college experiment ended. My natural father's death had left me with access to the GI Bill which paid my room and board, tuition, books and a few dollars extra. This I wasted by playing and barely getting by on a few classes. It was costing me nothing, and I valued it the same way. It would take another 25 years to finish the degree I walked away from. I also met a girl during this season. Girls at my high school wouldn't have much to do with me because I was a year younger (and an arrogant snot), but this one was a friend of my college roommates' girl back home. We started dating and with a lust inflamed brain; I asked her to marry. She dropped out of high school and I left college to make this happen. Neither family was happy. I asked Loyd to give me a job with the construction company he worked for. He did at minimum wage, and for a wedding gift, gave us a small increase in weekly salary. He should have fired me instead! The prodigal life was in full bloom now.

The marriage lasted just over three years. It is amazing how someone you can't bear to be apart from can become someone you can't bear to be with in a very short period of time. We soon discovered that reality. I was a pretty good provider, but not a good husband. I worked hard, often two jobs, overtime, side jobs and such. We discovered credit and paying on time. That is like doing prison time without the prison bars. You are still a prisoner to the lender. We fought over money, time spent with family, time together, what we didn't have and so on. Professionally, I did well, moving from construction to a job in a factory, and becoming joint manager of a convenience store. We thought the money would change our lives. It did. We spent more than we earned, fought about it often, and did not learn the lesson. The only good thing that came out of this season was a son. Like my father, I doted on him, but did not get the chance to see him grow up, or teach him the lessons of manhood (probably a good thing). One evening I returned home from my second job to hear the words "I want a divorce." I was stunned. While we fought and struggled, leaving the marriage had never entered my mind. We had made a "contract" and must see it through to the end. Divorce would mean I had failed as a man. Nothing I could say or do would change her mind, the wounding too great, the promise of perceived freedom too alluring, and we divorced. Still determined to solve life through my own strength, I willingly took the bulk of the expenses on myself. I swore I would not be an absentee father to my son. It took nearly eight years to liquidate the debt I had made, and the breach, between my son and I, has not yet been healed. Wasted, that is the word. DTime, a life together, finances, and many other things. Church was a thing of the past now, and the prodigal continued to unknowingly look for the end of himself.

For a short season, I would see my son at visitation times. I still remember him standing in the seat of my truck behind my right shoulder. Mandatory seat belts were not a thing in America yet. We enjoyed our time together; I think. It was one of the few times I would feel whole in this season. There was alcohol and anger and a fling with a married woman and all together I would wind up homeless and unemployed. So I did what anyone in my situation would do, I joined the Navy. I also made a vow in my heart that I would never again give myself entirely to a woman. I would never pay that price and lose everything again. Following my earlier life lessons about fists, I set off down the prodigal path determined to beat the world into submission, but it didn't work out that way. So, with a broken heart and a sack full of debt, I ran away to my Uncle Sam. In some ways, it turned out to be a good decision. I needed some discipline in my life. Got that! I had clothes, food, got more education, saw places I had never been and got paid for it. Bonus! I liked the work, Submarine duty paid extra, and the crew was like a big family of brothers. I decided within the first year to make it a career. To this day, I do not regret that decision. Not everything you do as a prodigal is necessarily bad. It is the sum total of all things that leads to the end of yourself.

About that time I would meet another woman. Didn't think much about it. She was living with a friend and I ate at their house a time or two. He was on a different sub than me, so I offered to be available to help if she needed while he was gone. It was an innocent "if you need the sink fixed, or a flat tire changed" offer. About 6 months later, the phone in the barracks would ring and it was for me. She was calling. My friend was at sea and she said he had been cheating on her. She wanted to talk. Yep, I fell for that one. We talked all night and into the daylight hours, but lust had begun to creep in. Such honor as remained in me would slip away over the next few weeks, and we would share an intimacy that should be reserved for marriage. I felt whole again, and guilty, and happy, and a lot of other emotions, none of which were Godly. Then deployment called, and I was gone. I thought of her often during the next three months, but when we returned to port, the house where they had lived was empty and she was gone, or so I thought.

A week would pass, and I received a letter from her. She had returned to the hills of Georgia and wanted to see me. She said she was free of other relationships. My heart soared, but my vow not to give myself away was still strong. We would talk with each other and I had some time off, so I went to her. During the visit, I would ask her to live with me. These were the conditions. She would have to work and pay half of our expenses. She could never ask me to leave the Navy. What kind of offer is that! She accepted and we would get an apartment together. We had a great summer in Charleston, SC and would decide to marry. The next two years were hot and cold. Shipyard overhaul kept me at home. Our brokenness would come out. The transfer had moved me away from my son so I could no longer visit him. She had lost children from an earlier divorce and grieved about it every holiday and on each child's birthday. I stuffed my loss in a box and she dumped her box of loss all over everyone, everywhere we went. It was maddening to me, but I had determined she could not have all of my heart, and equally determined we would make the marriage work. We survived that season, but we were not well.

The career was going well; I had been promoted twice and was now ahead of my peer group. That would remain the pattern for another 17 years, with 38 awards and medals in all. Promotion and recognition moving from enlisted to officer - now occupying a box in the bottom of a closet. But I had still not learned to be a good husband.

She would move to the next duty station ahead of the sub. That also would be a pattern, her doing the grunt work while I got the glory. In the meantime, at a party for the crew leaving the shipyard, with lots of beer, grilled steaks, a willing woman and shipmates egging me on, I broke my marriage vows. (In reality, this list of circumstances just allowed me to have an excuse to act out on my own lust.) The shame returned. And a new feeling - fear. Fear she would find out. For a place full of secret stuff, personal secrets are never secret on a sub. Having discussed my dilemma with someone I trusted for counsel, I decided to confess and hope for mercy. This was bad. I relieved my guilt and created a wounding that would last for decades. I made my problem her problem and wanted to be free of it; she wanted an explanation where none would suffice. Bad, bad, very bad. (Looking back, I don't recommend this approach without being in counseling together first. That way the confession is part of the growth and healing process.) Fortunately, God sent a miracle into our midst during this season. We adopted a newborn baby girl. The busyness of having an infant in the house distracted us from the struggles of living in the pigpen.

Children always bring joy and sorrow. For the most part, it was joy. But we were not healed. We decided to leave the pigpen and go to the field. Attending church seemed to improve things because we knew we were doing a good thing. Church makes everything all right, doesn't it? No, not really. So we squabbled and overspent and made up and promised to do better and we were in and out of church and the world for the next 7 years. I would continue to be successful in a career, she would take some comfort in that and the raising of our daughter. Sea duty came, and with it the strain of separation. Finally, it became too much. I arrived in Guam to a letter that said she was leaving. It broke me. The prodigal had found the pigpen and the end of himself. Success and reputation were falling apart, and the thought of being separated from the little girl was too much. So I turned towards Father's house. I did not try to fix it; I prayed and wept. She met me at the airport a few weeks later with the little girl. Told me it was over. She left. Said she would give me some time with our daughter while she sorted things out. I had time off, so I talked to the pastor of the church we had started attending and he gave me good advice. Repent of my sin, ask for forgiveness from God. Accept it when I ask. Make my petition to Him and let Him decide.

So I did. I prayed and read scripture - every verse I could find on marriage. After every positive thing I said "Lord, give me this in my life." About ten days passed and a call came. She wanted to come home. She had not yet met her pigpen, (people reach their pigpen when they reach it, timing is always unpredictable), but she was coming home, I believe, in answer to my prayers. The Father was watching and had begun to restore my life. There would be a lot of tension and struggle over the next two years, and I would continue to waffle between duty and the world. Finally, after a week of passing each other in the home without even speaking, we declared almost together, "If we don't get back to church, we will never make it." WE had now found our marriage pigpen and we could now go home together. (You are not forced to stay in the pen waiting on someone else. When you realize where you are, get up and get moving. This is just how it worked out in my life.) Church, by itself, was not the answer. Relationship with the

Father is the answer. Church attendance and participation only matter when they are a response to the love you are receiving from the Father. We sought counsel, changed church bodies, and found one that taught relationships. On our tenth anniversary, we renewed our vows in a recommitment ceremony. The marriage would last another twenty-eight years until her death.

I would like to say it was just that easy, but remember the part about the journey? Journeys can be filled with detours, traffic jams, breakdowns, wrecks and getting lost. It is in the journey that the relationship and trust in the Father is what matters, everything else is just passing through. And another thing, when the Father restored the younger son to the household, he did not give him back all that had been wasted. There is a consequence of sin. In my case, the loss of trust never completely healed and would manifest itself in times of difficulty. There is often a lifelong cost in the natural world for having been a prodigal. Nevertheless, returning to the Father will set your life in order, and whatever hardships must be endured are a small price to pay when compared to discovering the joy of a life filled with and surrounded by His presence. Don't wait any longer. Quit the pigpen and run home. The Father is waiting expectantly for your return.

Questions for Reflection

1. Can you identify with any of the challenges here? Does your life reflect the same or similar issues? What are they?

2. Do you acknowledge that you are a prodigal? How is that true?

3. What do you need to do to run towards home? When will you begin?

4. Will you accept that the penalty for your prodigal life has been fully paid for by the cross?

These questions are not accusations. They are challenges to reject our own selfishness and adherence to the world's standards and turn us towards home. It is my hope that you will see some of your life in mine and join me in the prodigal's journey home.

Chapter 3

From the Pigpen to the Salt Mine

(The Trap of Religion)

Galatians 4:8-9, Formerly, when you did not know God, you were enslaved to those that by nature are not gods. (9) But now that you have come to know God, or rather to be known by God, how can you turn back again to the weak and worthless elementary principles of the world, whose slaves you want to be once more?

Remember, in the story of the prodigal there is an elder brother. Having turned back to the Father, having received forgiveness and restoration, having learned of His grace and generosity, I did what any right thinking man would do. I set about trying to change myself to be the "good man" that so much of the Church says we must be. I was trying by strength of will and discipline to accomplish what can only be achieved by surrender and acceptance of grace, followed by submission to the daily leading of His Spirit. If being a prodigal was slavery to the world and its lust, then trying to serve God by being religious is slavery in a salt mine of never ending failure and accusation. I will try to share a few items so you may know what I am referring to.

First, religion asks you to perform. Attend, pray, fast, read, give, repent, and more. Now each of these things actually has a good basis. That is the prison of religion, things with a good basis done in man's strength and not the Spirit's leading. So I attended. If the doors were open, I was there. Work day, special meetings, extended services, community ecumenical events, yep, I made them all and after a while I resented it. Not that I resented God, or worship services, but I noticed the other "worthless sons" who did not attend, did not labor, missed special meetings, and I judged them unworthy and myself righteous. Both judgements were false. Church membership and gold star attendance earned me nothing. Any standing I had with God was freely given through His grace and paid for by Jesus' death on the cross.

I prayed and I felt guilty. First, I couldn't tarry for one hour. It was a burden to go 10 minutes. There was only so much begging, pleading and groveling, only so much asking and it all seemed so hopeless. If I prayed and it didn't turn out the way I expected, I would feel guilty that I had either not prayed enough, or I was unworthy because of my past. I tried pre-formatted prayers, reciting the prayers of others. None of that made a difference. In the end I felt God was far removed and I was throwing requests into the heavens hoping that something would stick. The guilt was back - God doesn't hear my prayers because I am sinful, lazy, selfish, pick your own adjective. Again, those feelings are all a lie.

I read and studied. Even that was hard. If I tried daily readings, something would happen and I would fall behind, or I would try to keep a reading plan. Didn't work for me. Then I felt guilty and ashamed. Why couldn't I love the scripture, why didn't I find joy in the reading, why did it seem foreign and stilted and stiff? I knew I needed to read the Bible, but found no joy in it. So, more guilt, feelings of worthlessness. Even memorization and quoting seemed powerless in my life.

Then there was my flesh. The pigpen side of me fought to return. I would repent and then find my mind wandering to the past and repent again. I felt dirty, broken, lost, and without hope. So I would fail, then I would repent, then I would attend and pray and study and...fail again. It was truly a salt mine slavery experience.

But I did not give up. I remembered the hopelessness and helplessness of the pigpen and continued to search for His way. Now the reality is, all of my efforts I described above are the world's way of approaching God. We think if we labor and strive and sacrifice, we will get His favor. In fact, of all the world's faith groups, only Christianity does not adhere to this "prove yourself" mentality. At its core, Jesus is saying, "Come as you are, I will receive you. Walk with Me and I will change you on the journey." We need to attend church meetings. YES! Regularly! And they should be a priority in our lives. In Hebrews 10 we are commanded to "not neglect to meet together." Why? Not as a measure of righteousness, but out of our deep need to receive from other travelers who will encourage us that this journey, though long and difficult, is worth the effort. We also have encouragement to bring to others. There is joy in traveling together and we need each other and that joy.

We need to read God's word. And memorize. And quote. And meditate. Psalms 1 encourages us to meditate day and night and promises reward for that diligence. Jesus himself, is referred to as the Word. It is not the number of verses, chapters or pages, it is the meditation, the pondering over and over in my mind the reality of this Word Jesus and the writings God has directed that slowly saturate my being and begin to bring change from the inside. It is the prayerful asking, "I do not understand Father, will you show me and teach me?" Learning to read the Bible not just as a book, but as a reference library for life was a revelation to me. As these scriptures get into my life and take root, they become a shield against the enemy's attack, a weapon to drive his temptations away, and a flame of wisdom for myself to follow and to be an encouragement to others. When a piece of scripture has been true in my life, I can then share that truth with others with confidence.

We must pray. But prayer is more than a petition. Prayer is more than "save me from this trouble I have gotten myself into." It is a living, ongoing conversation with a loving, living Father who longs to spend time with us. Prayer is worship and praise, interceding for others, giving thanks for His goodness, and yes, asking for our needs and even our wants to be met. It is a never ending chat with Dad, if we will let it be that. And it is joyful, not laborious. Jesus gave us a pattern with what we call "The Lord's Prayer." It begins "When you pray" (it is assumed that we will pray) "say" (it requires speaking and also listening). Prayer has become simple and natural, and I can help others along their journey by encouraging and praying with them.

So as not to bore the reader further, I will briefly highlight the next 30 years of my journey. I continued to move towards the Father and discovered several things. First, He really answers prayer. Not just whispering a wish variety of prayer covered with a pious "if it be thy will, O' Lord" which had been a staple in my life, usually related to getting me out of some trouble I had gotten myself into. Instead, I learned I could pray in faith according to His will with a confident expectation that He would move things in my life for my good and His glory. His answers often did not look like I expected they would, but He answered, again and again.

I discovered His promise for provision - enough and to spare. I experienced His moving in my finances, learned to give and trust and not be wasteful. No giant mystery gifts or million dollar miracles, just daily bread and a little extra every day. It worked when I was a plant supervisor with fifty employees in my charge and when I took a job as a school bus driver to allow me to care for ill family members. In all cases, we never missed a meal, never missed a bill, and while I was impatient to be debt free, He never was. He was constantly, steadfastly, generous. Finally, yielding our finances and following His lead, we finally got out of debt. It would take 20 years.

I would experience the depth of His forgiveness. Despite my anger towards Him, my selfish behavior, my being divorced and remarried, my living a sailor's life with all the negative things that are implied in that statement, He took me in and forgave me. The Bible's words were true!

Repentance and confession lead to forgiveness, a forgiveness you can feel and live. I am still amazed at the totality of His love. There I was covered in dirt, slop, and steeped in the smell of the pigpen and He covered it with a new robe. As with the finances, it would take years to fully embrace the forgiveness. I struggled to be worthy, hated myself for failure, declared "you can't use me" but He showed me otherwise. He sent me a mentor. Pastor Howard Ryan, who took time with the wreck that was me. When I recounted all the reasons for unworthiness listed above, he responded with, "so what." He had discovered that God would use who He chose to use, and it is better to cooperate with that than to resist it. He would later be the one used to reveal God's call on my life to minister and would guide me through part of the education and ordination process.

I would learn to love my wife and family, really love them by giving myself for them. The breakthrough came at a Promise Keepers' conference in 1996. Something in that stadium full of men was different. I came away broken within and yet at the same time healed. The judgmental self-righteousness was diminished and would largely disappear. I was no longer as important to me. The demand to "live like I say" was now replaced by His leading to walk together and become more like Jesus. That change was so needed, and later when the need to raise two grandchildren (ages 1 and 4) arose, I was ready. When my wife's health failed and I had to care for her, I was able. Yes, I wounded others and was wounded by them, and made mistakes - too many to count, and failed at times more miserably than you can imagine, but the overall picture was positive progress. Her final words to me were, "I worry about you. You work too hard taking care of me.

You love me too much!" The next morning she was gone. Quite a long way from the pigpen.

And ministry? That too was a journey. I studied and wrote a thesis and finished a Bachelors in Theology. I finished a Navy career and headed out to save the world, only to find doors that would not open. Like everything else, it was a journey of refinement, often with the fire of rejection and being beaten into shape with the hammer of reality. Finally, after twelve years of networking, and candidating, and handshaking and good old boy's clubs and letters of rejection, I declared to the Lord, "I guess I missed Your timing and calling for me in ministry. I lay it down. I am 52 and no one wants me so I will just stay here and be a blessing to my Pastor." I imagine now that God smiled and said, "finally, now I can use you." Six months later, I would be called to candidate for a church over a thousand miles distant. I would serve them as Pastor for nearly 12 years. It was the best time of my life to that point.

And personally? He cares about that too. In my widowerhood, as grief subsided and loneliness sought to enter its place, He sent a lovely, caring widow for me to love and marry. All the shaping, all the refining, all the learning to trust where He leads has borne fruit in this season of my life. We are in our fifth year of marriage and though some will roll their eyes; I declare to you we have not had a cross word between us in this entire season. Yes, we have differed in opinions, and made adjustments and concessions, but His presence has been with us. Neither of us had expectations of the fullness of joy we have received. A prophetic friend of ours, at my departure from the church pastorate, declared over us, "These are your glory days." It has been and continues to be true. So in these, my glory days, I am writing and traveling and filling in for those with need of me and walking closely with some on their journey and sharing my life's message. It is a joy.

Before I end this chapter, I would say that not everything in my life is perfect. I have a son who does not speak to me and grandchildren who do not know me. The door is open on my end. I have offered peace where it is mine to offer. The time will come. The Lord has promised this will be healed as well. I still struggle with feeling unqualified for His grace. I have a grandson in prison. It bothers me and I pray. I worry about how he will live when his time is up and I write and encourage him regularly. I also have the aches and pains and concerns of aging. But, in sum total, these are in fact my glory days.

Questions for Reflection

1. Does this chapter more closely identify your
    life? Are you a religious prodigal instead of
    a worldly one? If so, how can you move in
    repentance to enter the Father's house?

2. Do you resent attending services or giving in
    offerings or serving? Does it seem that
    church stuff gets in the way of life, or do
    you feel His leading or calling? Do the
    things where you sense His leading. Yes,
    attend and give and volunteer, but not
    everyone is called to do everything that
    needs doing. Listen for His voice and do
    those things where He leads.

3. Do you feel others are less spiritual because
    they do not do what you do? Let it go. They
    are responsible to the Father for their lives.
    We are responsible to build up and
    encourage them on the journey. It is freeing
    to let others live their own lives.

Chapter 4

A Beloved Son Well Pleasing to the Father

Matthew 3:17 and behold, a voice from heaven said, "This is my beloved Son, with whom I am well pleased."

This verse appears at the site of Jesus' baptism by John the Baptist. Jesus had submitted to John in humility and obedience to the Father and was publicly recognized as the "beloved of the Father." What if I told you that being a beloved son is God's plan for you and me as well?

In fact, I will do so now. You are a beloved son in whom God the Father is well pleased. I will say it again, with emphasis. **You are a beloved son in whom God the Father is well pleased.** I will offer scriptural proof of this in a moment, but before I do I want you to do something. Say this out loud. You don't have to believe it or even accept it, but before you read any further, say it aloud. "I, (your name) am a beloved son of God. He delights in me regardless of what I may or may not have done. His love for me is without regard to my current or former condition.

His love for me is unstoppable." Don't continue without doing this. This truth is the cornerstone for freedom from the lies of a prodigal life. It is in the understanding of how much He delights in us that we begin to experience true freedom on this journey. So write this down and read it to yourself and say it aloud until you can get it through your thick skull. He loves me regardless, and my sonship is secure.

Consider this:

Romans 8:29-30 For those whom he foreknew he also predestined to be conformed to the image of his Son, in order that he might be the firstborn among many brothers. (30) And those whom he predestined he also called, and those whom he called he also justified, and those whom he justified he also glorified.

And there it is. He has called us to believe in the work of Jesus on the cross and in so doing; He has named us who believe as brothers of Jesus. He being the first, and we following after in our season. Notice that the Father did not name us as step-brothers, half-brothers, foster brothers or some other such distinction, rather He names us as brothers on an equal footing with Jesus Himself. We are formed and shaped to look like Jesus to the world and to be carriers of His love and grace.

Paul, writing to the Ephesians, says we were chosen before time to be accepted in the beloved, to be adopted as sons, to be fellow heirs of the Kingdom of God. In this, one must first understand the Biblical concept of adoption. While there are no specific laws governing adoption, there are examples of it. Jacob adopted Joseph's sons, Ephraim and Manasseh, so he could give them a father's blessing. Moses was adopted by Pharaoh's daughter and was raised as a prince in Egypt. Esther was adopted and raised by her uncle Mordecai. Samuel was adopted into the family of Eli and raised as a priest and prophet of Israel. Even Jesus was adopted by Joseph and became submissive to him until adulthood. In these examples it should be noted that these sons and daughters became so because of the love, acceptance, and choice of the father. No legal rulings or court documents, simply the heart of the father opened to receive a child and keep them as heirs.

Some in this reading will have experienced adoption in the natural and the stigma that comes with it. Why didn't my birth parents want me? Why didn't they love me? What was wrong with me? These are the questions in the heart of a natural child. They may never be completely removed, but they can be overcome by the continuous application of love to the wounded heart. You are not unwanted, not damaged, not rejected, but you are chosen to be in a new and better circumstance. Stigma nullified!

In the same manner, the adoption of sons into the Kingdom of God brings its own set of questions. Why can't I keep the law? How can He forgive my sin when I can't? How does He not remember when I did (fill in your transgression here) that? I remember and am ashamed, how can He not be ashamed of me? And yet He assures us that we are free of the stigma of adoption and sin.

Consider this passage:

Psalms 103:10-13 He does not deal with us according to our sins, nor repay us according to our iniquities. (11) For as high as the heavens are above the earth, so great is his steadfast love toward those who fear him; (12) as far as the east is from the west, so far does he remove our transgressions from us. (13) As a father shows compassion to his children, so the LORD shows compassion to those who fear him.

This is a lot to absorb. My sin no longer matters! My prodigal wanderings do not count in the balance, nor does my religious hypocrisy. His love covers all that, and He is eager to show His compassion for us. I love the phrase "east from west." It is a deliberate choice of measure. If we go north far enough, we will eventually head south. It also works in reverse from south to north. But east and west, ahhh, that is different. No matter how far west you travel, you can continue going west and will never find yourself traveling east. That is the demonstration of how far He separates us from our failures and transgressions. Instead, He replaces it with His presence and His love.

Or this passage:

Micah 7:19 He will again have compassion on us; he will tread our iniquities underfoot. You will cast all our sins into the depths of the sea.

In our natural world, the deepest part of the sea is more than two miles deeper than the tallest mountain peak. It is a practical picture of how He considers our sin behind or removed from us. He walks over them to get to us and to save us from them. Truly, we are beloved sons.

But, you may ask, what is a son really? Is it one born from a man's seed? One chosen from a group to be part of the family? One who inherits the life work of the father? It could be all of these, or none of them, or some combination. The Greeks had multiple words for sons and we will look at three **huios**, **teknon**, and **pais**. Each of these words translated as son is based on the context in which it is used. Understanding these will help us understand our relationship to God the Father.

Huios - a son (pronounced whee-ose). A male child of the father and legitimately an heir. It is contrasted with the word *nothos*, which refers to an illegitimate son. **Huios** is the word God chose when He announced Jesus' sonship in Matthew 3:17. It is also the word chosen to describe the adoption of Moses by Pharaoh's daughter in Acts 7:21. And perhaps most significantly, it is the word used in Romans 8:14.

Romans 8:14-17 For all who are led by the Spirit of God are sons of God. (15) For you did not receive the spirit of slavery to fall back into fear, but you have received the Spirit of adoption as sons, by whom we cry, "Abba! Father!" (16) The Spirit himself bears witness with our spirit that we are children of God, (17) and if children, then heirs—heirs of God and fellow heirs with Christ, provided we suffer with him in order that we may also be glorified with him.

Just as the Holy Spirit overshadowed Mary, causing her to conceive Jesus, the Christ, so the Holy Spirit, in response to our confession of faith, enters our hearts to birth sonship in us. So here we have the greek **huios**, our sonship laid out in scripture. We are called the same word "sons" as the Son Jesus. Our adoption is covered by the Spirit using the same word. Then, our sonship is announced that we are children of God. So in all aspects of the Father's involvement, we are sons of God. He claims us and calls us His own. He provides an inheritance for us and proclaims us as joint heirs of the Kingdom with His Son Jesus. Yes, we are sons; sons that He delights in! Unfortunately, this is the sonship we are most comfortable with. It is the sonship that says I get, I receive, I have the benefits of being a son of my father. What it lacks is intimacy.

Romans 8:16-17 introduces the second word of sonship, *Teknon* - true children, genuine descendants. As **huios** indicates the legal lineage of sonship, **teknon** describes the emotional attachment in the parent child relationship. **Huios** is a word of position and authority, **teknon** is a word of relationship, care and compassion. Some additional definitions include "one who is the object of parental love and care" and "a tender term of address, equivalent to "my child" or "my son." God the Father does not just consider us as heirs with Jesus, but as true sons, sons of His affection, sons of His provision, protection and care. I believe we are the sons that He points to and says to the angels, "that's My Boy!" **Teknon** is the word chosen for the oldest son when the father begged him to come in to the celebration for his brother. **Huios** is used for the younger son throughout the story. The communication, "my heritage son has returned, but my relational son, won't you come celebrate with me?" A **teknon** can enter the father's joy. A secondary indication of the relational aspect of this word is our response, "Abba Father." Abba is the Greek transliteration of a Hebrew word meaning father. In the New Testament, abba is always used in relation to God and in conjunction with the greek word *pater,* meaning Father. So when hearing this, the people of the day would have understood the double father reference to be a reference of relationship, such as My Father. In our day we might say the more relational Daddy God. Truly, that is the cry of sons that are well pleasing to Him. **Teknon** is a step closer to the heart of God. But there is yet another level of sonship, servanthood.

Pais - is an interesting word because it refers to a child as in Luke 2:43 where the "child" Jesus stayed behind at the temple, and in such usage it indicates sonship, relationship, and inheritance, but there is a broader usage and understanding. It also means servant, or slave, and in relation to Jesus is used several times to invoke the suffering servant aspect of His ministry. The word appears 24 times with 10 uses as son or child and 10 uses as servant. It is largely interchangeable when understood as the relationship of a son who provides a service for the father. It also indicates one in whom authority is invested to accomplish the will of the father. It is here in the *pais* relationship that we will live most of our earthly time. The place of sonship and servanthood in a combined life, a son of service. Paul's letter to the Galatians explains this.

Galatians 4:1-7 I mean that the heir, as long as he is a child, is no different from a slave, though he is the owner of everything, (2) but he is under guardians and managers until the date set by his father. (3) In the same way we also, when we were children, were enslaved to the elementary principles of the world. (4) But when the fullness of time had come, God sent forth his Son, born of woman, born under the law, (5) to redeem those who were under the law, so that we might receive adoption as sons. (6) And because you are sons, God has sent the Spirit of his Son into our hearts, crying, "Abba! Father!" (7) So you are no longer a slave, but a son, and if a son, then an heir through God.

We who believe in Jesus are sons! We are heirs! We are also servants entrusted to work for and in the Kingdom to accomplish God's purpose on earth in our lives and the lives of those we come in contact with. We are adopted, chosen, and in relationship with the Spirit of Jesus in our heart calling out "My Father." And while we serve, we are not slaves but sons! Sons in whom God the Father has a great delight.

So we can see that sonship is a key theme in scripture, but what does it look like in our lives? I will give you an example from the story of my life.

Until my 14th year I was both **huios** and **teknon** - a son and heir in a special relationship with my natural father. I was his buddy, his mini-me, his delight. Then he died, and I felt orphaned. Two years later, my mother would meet and marry another man. As I described in an earlier chapter, I was 16 and rebelled against the thought of another father. And yet he claimed me as a son, **huios** a son in standing and a descendant and heir. I would accept that relationship but reject being a **teknon**. He on the other hand persisted and loved me, anyway. He loved me by treating my siblings as his own and by loving my mother richly and truly in a way that was obvious. He gave me wisdom and counsel even when I ignored it. After some ten years, I let myself become a teknon in his life. I accepted and returned the affection offered. Then I sought out his counsel and wisdom, and it was given freely. The day came when I asked him to lay his hands on my head and pray a father's blessing over my life. He did, with tears, asking God to fulfill His purposes in me, to keep me and guide me until this life was over. That prayer is still being lived out in my life. Then the final change came. I was visiting him in the hospital and he needed help to get his pants down for a bathroom trip. There, I felt the frailty of a man who had been strong in his youth. My transition to **pais** had begun. I served largely by visiting and conversation. Providing companionship in the evenings, sitting out and drinking coffee. Bringing two little boys to see "Big Papa." It was a delight in his life seeing them. He always loved children. Finally, I served by officiating at his home-going. Sharing his life story and witness from one who had lived it. I didn't understand then what I see so clearly now, how he was God the Father lived out in human form in my life. To him I was **huios**, **teknon**, and **pais**. My life is richer for it. At the end, I knew I was a beloved son, well pleasing to my father.

You may never have experienced this. In fact, your life may be the opposite, but God in His mercy will send fathers to the fatherless in the form of men in your life. I will cover this in more detail in the chapter on fathers, but if you look carefully back over your life, there have been fathers God has placed for you to make up for your earthly fathers shortcomings. Included in this list is Grandfathers, uncles, brothers, cousins, school bus drivers, coaches, boot camp instructors, supervisors on the job and more. The list is unending and the Father of fathers is reaching out to you through them. Look for His hand in the men you know, you will find it.

Finally, being a son means we have an inheritance. Here and in the life to come! There are over 300 direct references to inheritance, blessing, and favor related to being an heir of God. I will highlight a few. Psalm 24:5 - Righteousness - we inherit a standing with the Father that eliminates all that is or has ever been ungodly in our lives. Psalm 127:3 - Children - remember we are inheriting the Kingdom. More than natural children, we will have children in the faith. I have many more who call me a father in the faith than those who call me father in the flesh. What a joy to receive a call or a text that says, "What do you think? What is the Lord saying?" Sons in the Kingdom are our heritage. Matthew 16:19 - Keys to the Kingdom - authority in the Kingdom. The authority to declare His word as a son, to enter His presence in prayer, to find His favor in the most improbable of places. Luke 12:32 - The Kingdom Itself - this verse says it is His pleasure to give this to us. Our inheritance, if you will, is out of this world. Psalm 37:4 - Desires of our heart - when our sonship moves to seeking His Kingdom, our inheritance is Him replacing our desires with His desires for us. In this new place of desire, we seek and then find His fulfillment as our inheritance.

I have gone into a bit of detail hoping to prove that sonship is a journey. There is that which is imparted **huios**, that which is given in return **teknon**, and finally that which only comes from a heart of love where we empty ourselves in response to his calling forth sons **pais**. To love the Father as He loves us is a journey, a gift, and is also a key to the rest of our lives. You see, until we become the **pais** sons of service, we can never be the brothers and fathers we are meant to be. Sonship is the foundation for this lifelong journey.

If you catch nothing else, latch on to these two keys about being a beloved son. Being a beloved son requires the Father to accept and love you. In our case, the love of God the Father was never lacking and always available. Even more so, the acceptance is there to come as we are. We are accepted in the work of Jesus to come as we are, but not stay as we are. Secondarily, it requires my acceptance of the work of Jesus and submission to the leading of the Holy Spirit in order to receive the fullness of life as a son of my Father. God has done His part perfectly, all things are prepared for my life as His son. Will I step into it?

Questions for Reflection

1. Have you taken the step to become **huios,** a son who inherits? This happens when we accept the work of Jesus the Christ, on the cross. If you have not, this is the first step. Find a pastor, Sunday school teacher, men's group leader, or even someone you know to be a Christian and ask them to explain the prayer of faith and salvation. Then pray that prayer and you will be a **huios**. (Check our Appendix A)

2. Have you moved from **huios** to **teknon**? Do you find joy in scripture, worship, prayer, and fellowship with believers? If not, pray and ask the Father to show you by His Spirit what things are holding you back. Reject thoughts of unworthiness and guilt. You are a beloved son in whom He is well pleased. Let your love extend back to Him.

3. Have you embraced the call to be **pais**? The servant son. It is here we find ourselves laying aside the pursuits of the world for the pursuits of the Kingdom. It does not mean we have no concern in this world, this world is our temporary home. It does however mean that the cry of our heart is to reveal the Kingdom here and rejoice in it when we arrive there.

4. Do you accept that all of this life is a journey to the next? None of these things, salvation, church membership, tithing, prayer, scripture reading, and too many others to name, are a destination. They are only wayside stops where we pause for refreshing and get acclimated to our new status before we push off on the next part of the journey. Step out with Him and keep on stepping.

Chapter 5

The Bonds of Brotherhood

Proverbs 17:17 A friend loves at all times, and a brother is born for adversity.

    Lord of the Rings, The Hobbit, Saving Private Ryan, Star Wars, The Dirty Dozen, Jesus and the Twelve, what do these things have in common? While most are fiction and one is not, they are the stories that men truly love. The story goes something like this. A great evil has arisen or a great injustice has been done that must be righted. A quest is planned, but it can only be undertaken by a few. No great armies, just a band of misfits and malcontents out to save the world through a heroic rescue. They are outnumbered, over matched, ill-equipped and suffer hardships as they journey. They fight among themselves, worry about the hopelessness of the cause, struggle to find the courage, but inevitably they press on to a great and final battle to win it all. Opportunity comes to quit, to break the bonds of fellowship, to leave the captured to their fate, and each time it is rejected. No man left behind, they press on to blow up the death star, kill Smaug the dragon and defeat Azog the defiler, destroy the ring of power in the fires of Mount

Doom, rescue the last remaining son of Mrs. Ryan, Defeat Satan by the Cross and introduce the Church Age. It is heroic, epic, thrilling, and I want to play a part in the great story. So do you. I have good news for you. We are part of the greatest story ever told, and we have a significant place in that story. Our part will be revealed as we enter the Bonds of Brotherhood.

I love these stories and a hundred more like them. Even now, as I approach my 70th year, my heart quickens at the sound of a great adventure. I remember my own life and adventures and still thrill to them. Swimming in the creek with cottonmouth moccasins laying under trees nearby. Camping and fishing. Playing sports. Joining the Navy. Becoming part of the elite, the Submarine Service. Taking a brand new sub to sea and diving it for the first time, hoping everything would work, but glad to be there. Being called to ministry, moving 1000 miles to be a first time pastor at age 53. Seeing people come to the Lord, lives being changed. Experiencing things that made my former life adventures pale in comparison. Most recently, finding the wife God prepared for my old age because He knew that Bob alone was "not good." The adventure continues with great joy.

It is not just my own story that thrills me. When I was a senior pastor, I would slip unknown into groups of men at conferences with a "Hi, I'm Bob." And sit with guys I didn't know just to hear their story. When they didn't know who I was, was when the best stories were told. As soon as one of my guys would show up and call me pastor, the stories dried up. We are all too self-conscious about our own lives. **WE** all have a story to tell and we need to tell it.

I mentioned the trials along the way, and I have had my own. Divorced once, widowed, buried an infant granddaughter, an adult daughter, lost contact with grandchildren when my own children went through divorce, and all the stuff that happens to people in life. Yet, it has been an adventure and joyous journey. And a large part of this joy comes from having been bonded with my brothers along the way. Let's look at some scripture and stories together.

A quick view of scripture shows God's plan for brotherhood repeatedly. Abraham had Lot, Moses had Aaron. David and Johnathan became such close brothers that Johnathan betrayed his father Saul for his bonded brother David. Throughout scripture, you find the key figure in the story and then the one God sent with them. Moses sent twelve spies into Canaan and Joshua sent two. David had a group of 30 or more mighty men, brothers every one. Jesus sent the 12 and then the 70 out by twos. God called out Barnabas and Saul. Saul, now Paul, took Silas. Barnabas took John Mark. The Epistles always list those who are laboring with Paul. We are made to be brothers and we need to have brothers.

Ecclesiastes 4:9-12 (9) Two are better than one, because they have a good reward for their toil. (10) For if they fall, one will lift up his fellow. But woe to him who is alone when he falls and has not another to lift him up! (11) Again, if two lie together, they keep warm, but how can one keep warm alone? (12) And though a man might prevail against one who is alone, two will withstand him—a threefold cord is not quickly broken.

It is believed Solomon wrote this in his old age. The rich King of Israel, who had everything and everyone at his disposal, the one in whom God had placed all the wisdom of man, still noted that he needed someone else in his life on a personal level. In fact, in the reading of all names and officials, we find this gem. *1 Kings 4:5 Azariah the son of Nathan was over the officers; Zabud the son of Nathan was priest and **king's friend;*** (emphasis mine). Zabud was assigned to be the King's friend. Even the King needed someone to open up to - to share his thoughts and ideas, hopes, dreams, and even his disappointments. The Hebrew meaning here indicates one who has a personal attachment to another. They have insight and understanding of the deepest secrets and support and promote the cause of their friend.

Jesus gives us similar insight into His own life. At the last supper, on the last night he would spend with the disciples before His crucifixion, He said this. *John 15:15 No longer do I call you servants, for the servant does not know what his master is doing; but I have called you friends, for all that I have heard from my Father I have made known to you.* After three years together, He revealed completely who they were to Him. He waited to give this revelation until after Judas had left! Then He told them, I have told you everything and held nothing back from you. Later in the evening He would scold them for falling asleep during the garden prayer. He wanted the support of their company and engagement for a task that only He could complete. That is friendship.

I know it may seem I have drifted off topic, but being a friend is a key component of being a brother. Returning to Ecclesiastes, *two are better than one* because they are more effective together. Think about any number of tasks. One may have the lead, such as a brain surgeon - you only want one set of hands reaching into the skull, but many will be there to assist. The various assisting doctors and nurses keep focus, monitor progress, provide encouragement and strength to the one doing the task. Brothers who are friends join with us in the work of life and help us complete or advance in the tasks.

If they fall, they will help each other up. Did you ever take a fall in deep snow, mud, or maybe on ice. If you have, you know how difficult it can be to get out of that circumstance, but with a brother extending a hand, it becomes easier. So it is in our Christian walk. First understand that we will fall. Micah 7:8 makes this clear but tells us that falling is neither fatal nor final. We can and must get back up. Paul's writings take it farther than that.

Galatians 6:1-2 Brothers, if anyone is caught in any transgression, you who are spiritual should restore him in a spirit of gentleness. Keep watch on yourself, lest you too be tempted. (2) Bear one another's burdens, and so fulfill the law of Christ.

Brothers, he writes. It is the duty of brothers to take up the part of the fallen, to restore gently, not approving of the failing, or excusing it, but calling the fallen one up to a higher level in Christ. Doing so while holding them firmly to prevent them from falling again. Gentleness does not remove the necessity of tough love. It does however remove guilt, shame and condemnation from the restoration process. A brother can counsel sternly and lovingly at the same time. I have a son named Tony, some would say a stepson because he came into my life at the ripe age of 21, within a few months of meeting him, I sat him down and read him the riot act about what it means to be a man and how to take care of your family and children and what your responsibilities are. Shortly after, he would leave us again and go on his own path. But the message stuck. This year on Father's Day, when he talked with me, he recounted that conversation. "Dad, he said, I hated you in that conversation. It was the worst butt whipping I ever had in my life. But it stuck with me. I am over 50 years old and that changed me. Thank you." Truth, even hard truth in love, is life changing and all too rare in our society today.

Also, we must watch our own lives. The mud that caught our brother is grasping at our feet, trying to pull us down as well. The word *bear,* besides meaning carry or lift up or support, may also include to "endure with patience." Brothers have to put up with some stuff from each other. Often things we would rather avoid or just get rid of. Draw close and put your shoulder to the load. It will not be as heavy as you think if your heart is filled with love for your brother.

Keeping warm together fits with the above paragraph. The obvious reference is to sleeping outside with little or no shelter and sharing body heat. Soldiers will tell you that the center guy in the foxhole sleeps best because he is warm on both sides and his brothers are keeping guard. We need to adapt this to our lifestyle. Let my fire for Christ and the Kingdom give warmth when you are feeling challenged and stressed or your faith feels weak. In the same manner, when I am weak, I can be warmed by the Kingdom's passion in your life. You have seen this work. Some brother speaks of what God is doing in his life, and you become stirred inside. I draw strength when I see God using my brothers, because I know He has not given up on them or me.

Last, Solomon writes of the need for brothers in a fight. Two can hold off an enemy's attack and a *threefold cord* is not quickly broken. When we get in a battle, or when we fall, the enemy is quick to come in on the attack. He will bring words like "you are worthless, you are no good, Jesus is wasting His time with you." I've heard these things and likely you have too, or words like them. A brother will step in to lift us up. Maybe sharing a struggle from their own life, or reminding us of a scripture, or keeping watch with us in prayer as the Spirit works His renewal in our lives. And where two are powerful, three are almost impossible for the enemy to overcome. Why? Because Jesus gives us these great promises.

Matthew 18:18-20 "Truly, I say to you, whatever you bind on earth shall be bound in heaven, and whatever you loose on earth shall be loosed in heaven. (19) Again I say to you, if two of you agree on earth about anything they ask, it will be done for them by my Father in heaven. (20) For where two or three are gathered in my name, there am I among them."

There is great power in prayer, meditation and study of scripture together, also in the seeking of God's will for a certain item. I have seen numerous things turned around at the eleventh hour through prayer. Here is a brief story of one such time.

Larry (not his actual name) was struggling in his marriage when he came to me. He was a believer and faithful attender in our church. His wife had struggled with drugs off and on and was now in the *on* phase. When he resisted, she got a court order and filed for divorce, blocking him from the home and his children for being "abusive." This was not a thing I had ever observed from him, and most who knew him thought it false. Still, she had the court, the home, the children, and the most crooked lawyer I had ever known. After some months of counseling with him, he approached me and said, "I am not going to court. I am going to seek God in prayer and give myself into His hands. This was two weeks before the court date. I agreed to pray with him, which we did and fasted for that season. On the thirteenth day, she was caught in a major drug sting. Her lawyer dropped the suit and Larry got his home and the kids returned. His wife was sentenced to a long-term treatment facility and got the help she needed. They eventually got back together.

Not all things work out as spectacularly as this, but many do. Others work out slowly over time. Some seem to not change at all, but men in prayer are changed by the time spent together. The point is the prayers of brothers together are powerful and effective. They can withstand the enemy that seeks to destroy us and separate us from God. Prayer with our brothers is one way God uses to shape and mold us in the image of Jesus.

Not all brotherly relationships are uplifting and encouraging. Brothers can fight with each other like rabid animals. But don't try to break them up or pick a fight with one or the other of them. You will have to whip them both if you do, and that is like falling in a wood chipper. There are teeth everywhere! But true brotherhood, brothers that are bound together in purpose, will have confrontations about keeping each other on track. Look at these passages.

Galatians 2:11-13 But when Cephas came to Antioch, I opposed him to his face, because he stood condemned. (12) For before certain men came from James, he was eating with the Gentiles; but when they came he drew back and separated himself, fearing the circumcision party. (13) And the rest of the Jews acted hypocritically along with him, so that even Barnabas was led astray by their hypocrisy.

Cephas (Peter) was a leader in the Jerusalem Church and the first one sent to the Gentiles. But his behavior made him look like a hypocrite. Paul called him out publicly in order to protect the Gentile believers and return Peter to righteousness. A brother will bring correction.

Acts 15:37-39 Now Barnabas wanted to take with them John called Mark. (38) But Paul thought best not to take with them one who had withdrawn from them in Pamphylia and had not gone with them to the work. (39) And there arose a sharp disagreement, so that they separated from each other. Barnabas took Mark with him and sailed away to Cyprus.

Now look who the hypocrite is. Paul lacked the grace to restore John Mark to the work because of Mark's previous behavior. Barnabas took Mark's part to the point that he (the one who had gone after Paul to bring him into the church) now parted from one brother in order to save another. Later, when Paul wrote some of his last letters to

Timothy, he asked that Mark be sent to him because he was now useful to the ministry.

Mark 9:33-35 And they came to Capernaum. And when he was in the house he asked them, "What were you discussing on the way?" (34) But they kept silent, for on the way they had argued with one another about who was the greatest. (35) And he sat down and called the twelve. And he said to them, "If anyone would be first, he must be last of all and servant of all."

We think of the twelve as great men in the faith, and so they were, but sometimes all of us need to be humbled just a bit. This reminder got them back on the mission. What reminders do we need today?

Proverbs 27:5-6 Better is open rebuke than hidden love. (6) Faithful are the wounds of a friend; profuse are the kisses of an enemy.

This passage gives us the test of true brotherhood. Are my brothers willing to confront me when I need confronting? Will they receive corrections from me? The reality is each of us needs someone who will hold us accountable. Someone who loves us, but is not overly impressed by us. Someone willing to warn us of the pitfalls, tell us we are drinking too much, cheating on our spouse, neglecting the scripture. Whatever the flaw is, the enemy will draw us away if he can, but a true brother will try to pull us back and save us from our own folly.

Proverbs 27:17 Iron sharpens iron, and one man sharpens another.

This brings me to the end of what brotherhood looks like. Iron sharpening iron. Think about sports teams. During the pre-season, the A-team will practice against the B-team to get the timing right on plays, shake off the rust, and limber up the skills. They are tested by the B-team, but not really challenged or strengthened. But when the season gets close, the A-team offense goes against the A-team defense. Now they are being tested. And the B-team? Well, they are strengthened by going against the A's. It all works to build the team into a stronger unit.

Military training uses this same philosophy. You are training the one who will be watching your back. How well do you want your back watched? The special forces people and snipers have incredibly difficult training just to get in. Then when you are in, the training continues, constantly sharpening your skills to make you the best you can be. Why is this? The strength of the group is only as strong as the strength of the weakest member. When I entered Submarine Service I had graduated first in my boot camp, Second in my technical school, and 6th in my sub school class of 150. It did not matter in the first boat. I was the new guy and not to be trusted with anything. But they would teach me, one on one, hands on experience, walking with me, correcting and guiding until one day I passed the board - answered all the questions right and was awarded a pair of Silver Dolphins. Less than 2% of the Navy is in that group. I was part of the elite. But the training continued, and I now was responsible for training others. Someone failing to shut a valve, close a watertight door, throw the right switch at the right time could send us all to the ocean bottom. We were brothers and remain so to this day because we trusted each other with our lives.

We love the stories of heroes. Individual acts of heroism come from the group dynamic of brotherhood. This dynamic is where you learn to value your brother's life more than your own. The one who falls on a grenade, risks enemy fire to save a comrade, or the one charging a machine gun nest to save his unit pinned down by fire. Those guys are already dead to themselves. If you could visit wounded men at Walter Reed or Bethesda military hospitals, you would hear the same question asked repeatedly. "Doc, when can I go back to my unit?" This question often comes from men who have lost eyes, limbs, part of their face is burned off and other such tragic injuries. They want to be back, not denying their injury, but instead desiring to protect their brothers from the same. These guys are dead to themselves as well.

It's not just the military. It is firefighters who enter burning buildings. Police who seek to stop an active shooter while outgunned and exposed. These heroes put their safety aside and let the lives of others come to the center of their actions. They have died to themselves in that moment and placed the lives of others to the greater importance.

Finally you find this in church. Well, in churches where preaching about Christ is illegal. This level of commitment is seldom found in the American church because we have too much freedom. Pastor preached something I don't like, I will find another church. Or I will find a mega-church where I can hide in the masses. Get just enough of Jesus to die a comfortable death in my sin and wake up in hell. Our culture is changing now. The day may come that to wear the label Christian is to paint a target on your back. I pray it doesn't but I prepare for it in case it does.

Luke 9:23-24 And he said to all, "If anyone would come after me, let him deny himself and take up his cross daily and follow me. (24) For whoever would save his life will lose it, but whoever loses his life for my sake will save it."

Sunday services are where you get encouraged to come to Jesus. Encouraged to live your life for Him. We need Sunday service and our greater church body. Mid-week classes or small groups are where you get equipped with the knowledge to live the life. But where you learn to die to self is in the actual living. Brothers help with that. If you have never given regularly to the church, learning to do so is dying to self. Giving up activities that may not be evil in themselves in order to live the Christ life, is dying to self. Each step will cost us something until eventually it will cost everything of us, but in return He gave us all of Himself. We win. We die in stages and I will expand that more in the *Journey* chapter. The point is having brothers who have died to themselves in order to give, pray, study, witness - these are mighty men who will help you on your journey.

Now that we see the necessity of brothers, how do we go about finding them? Two ways primarily. God sends them to you and God sends you to them. Here are some examples of each.

1 Samuel 22:1-2 David departed from there and escaped to the cave of Adullam. And when his brothers and all his father's house heard it, they went down there to him. (2) And everyone who was in distress, and everyone who was in debt, and everyone who was bitter in soul, gathered to him. And he became commander over them. And there were with him about four hundred men.

David was running for his life from his father-in-law, Saul, the King of Israel. He was hiding in the cave or stronghold in an area called Adullum and God sent him men, distressed, indebted, bitter-hearted men. As I would say broke, busted and disgusted. Notice something here. On our journey God will send us others, learning the same lessons, so that our iron can be sharpened. These men became warriors and the core of David's army as more people left Saul and joined him. 1 Chronicles 12:1-22 contains the list of heroes that arose out of the four hundred and records some of their heroic deeds. This rag-tag group became crack troops as their leader David worshipped and wept his way through about 15 years of history on his way to finally becoming King. God will send us the men we need to grow with if we look for it. They may come in ones and twos or in a men's group. When a potential brother asks you to a meal, a cup of coffee, for prayer and study or to watch a ball game, pay attention. God may be sending the very man you need at the time you need him.

Others God will send to you are those looking for Him. They may see something new in your life. Or see something they desire. The number of different ways they approach you is too numerous to list here, but be sure, if you are following Jesus, others are watching and some will come wanting to follow as well.

John 1:40-41 One of the two who heard John speak and followed Jesus was Andrew, Simon Peter's brother. (41)

He first found his own brother Simon and said to him, "We have found the Messiah." (which means Christ).

John 1:45 Philip found Nathanael and said to him, "We have found him of whom Moses in the Law and also the prophets wrote, Jesus of Nazareth, the son of Joseph."

Here are two examples of someone recently finding the treasure of knowing Jesus and going and telling their own brother first. It may not be our natural brothers, but the principle is the same. Those we know who need to know who Jesus is; God is sending us to them even now. We may have to go several times. Extend multiple invitations. Pray numerous prayers. And most importantly, live a changed life always, so they begin to ask questions of you. When they do ask, you can be ready with testimony of what Jesus' death on the cross did for you and how being a beloved son of God and now being bonded to your spiritual brothers has changed your life.

There is one more group being sent for, nomad brothers. God sends us to bring those who are believers wandering and separated from a local assembly into the brotherhood. Some of this group have been hurt or wounded by church people. They are offended and hard to be won back. We must gently go after and seek to draw them into the brotherhood. It can be a long slow process, but their healing is worth it. Then, there are those who have gained a salvation experience apart from a church congregation, maybe at a conference, or praying a prayer with a radio broadcast, or reading a Gideon Bible. I know a brother and fellow minister who tells of getting saved on the street under a one-way sign. He was walking, and the Spirit called to him there. Another man came to know God under a tree in the woods with no one else around. They both responded to teachings and tellings without someone being physically present when they surrendered. Though their future is secure, their present self, needs to be healed and strengthened and we, in turn, have a need for the strengthening they will provide.

Consider this passage:

Acts 11:25-26 So Barnabas went to Tarsus to look for Saul, (26) and when he had found him, he brought him to Antioch. For a whole year they met with the church and taught a great many people. And in Antioch the disciples were first called Christians.

Saul, prosecutor of the Church in Acts 8, captured by a new revelation of Jesus on the road to Damascus in Acts 9, is now preaching in synagogues and among the Gentiles. The Jerusalem church is unsure, and Barnabas is sent to investigate. He then brings Saul to the church at Antioch where they minister together. In time, Saul becomes Paul and also becomes the pre-eminent preacher from that church, planting numerous churches and writing about two-thirds of the letters in the New Testament. Because Barnabas took a chance, became a brother, and invited an outside believer (Saul), great things happened. Now, I don't expect any of us to find a Saul, but we could find a Billy Graham or someone like him.

This is where I am in my life. God sends men to me to add them to the brotherhood. To welcome and shepherd them on their journey. He also sends me after those that know Him but are apart from Him. Although I am in church weekly, and preach often at various locations, I think the most effective part of my ministry is done around a campfire or leaning on the back of a pickup truck. I pray with and for men in the parking lot and at the hardware store, and most importantly follow up with a text message or phone call and an invitation to get together again. Brothers need companionship and fellowship. We also need someone to prod us to get moving towards each other.

There is a third finding of brothers I will mention lightly here because it is more rare. Start a men's fellowship yourself. Not a Bible study or a prayer group, although study and prayer will be part of the process. Instead, start a fellowship group. I am moving into the third year of a fellowship group here. We meet once a month from May through October at my home. Outside around the fire pit, enjoying hot meat from the grill, these men share their lives and struggles. They pray for and encourage each other and I do bring a short lesson, currently from the life of David. The premise of this book was born in this group from the first year's fellowship. It is not a detailed study but "take a look at this verse" and "let's apply this to our lives." The group has grown from four to eight, with some scattered visits from potential brothers checking us out. You should get your pastor's permission, I did. (He will most likely give it gladly.) At the end of it all, brotherhood forms in connection and men connect better around food and fire for the most part. (I have found that a 300 pound man is comfortable in a group of strangers if you give him a pulled pork sandwich and a Coke.) Common ground starts fellowship and we men all like to eat.

Finally, I would issue a few warnings about brothers. As much as we need them and even want them, not all men can or will be our brothers. Snipers and jet jockeys don't run in the same circles. As much as possible, be a brother and encourage all men on their journey. Some men come scarred from life. Others tattooed and pierced. These are marks of their journey and battle to be where they are. Often they have battled alone. Don't let meeting you be another battle over what is proper for Christians to look like externally. Men will often come and go several times before committing to or rejecting a group. Most do. Those that stay form the circle of brotherhood for you. Even within that circle there is a cautionary tale. Not all of your brothers are trustworthy. Cain killed Abel over something God said. Jacob stole Esau's birthright. Joseph's brothers threw him in a pit and sold him to slavery. Judas walked with Jesus for three years and was the treasurer of the group, implying that he had their trust. But scripture notes that he was a thief and stole from the bag of the treasury. Let them in anyway. Their lives may change because of Christ's presence in you. You also will not be able to share all of your deepest hurts or dreams with your circle. At this season in my life I have about three or maybe four men with whom I would feel comfortable opening up the depths of my heart and letting them look in and impart wisdom. None of these men attend my current church or the men's group I lead. That includes my pastor, although I could and would share most things with him. He has been my pastor for just over three years, so it is progress. Guard your heart and draw close to your brothers.

Take this with you. We were made for brothers. We need brothers. We must be bound to some of our brothers so that we learn how to lose our lives for their sake and ours. God sends some to us and others He sends us after. Some will be close to our heart like Johnathan and David, and others will be like Judas. We should embrace and encourage them, anyway. We don't always know which is which. I think a man's life is balanced when he has three brothers in it. A Timothy, a younger man I am building my life into. A Barnabas, a man my equal who loves me, knows me, and will call me out when I need it. And a Paul, a mature man who through his journey with the Lord imparts and builds into my life. Look for these guys. Get bonded. Welcome to brotherhood.

Questions for Reflection

1. Do you see and understand the scriptural call to brotherhood? Write some of the reasons for brotherhood here and think about them. Is that happening in my life?

2. Are you bonded to brothers? If not, why not? What would it take to move into brotherhood?

3. Where are you on the path to brotherhood? Seeking? Entered in? Bonded? Leading? We should all be there somewhere. If not, what is keeping you from embarking on this journey?

4. Write down some of the things you have received from brotherhood. Write the good and the bad. These things become part of your testimony. (See Appendix B)

Chapter 6
Benevolent Fathers

1 Corinthians 4:15-16 (15) For though you have countless guides in Christ, you do not have many fathers. For I became your father in Christ Jesus through the gospel. (16) I urge you, then, be imitators of me.

(Authors Note: Before we enter this topic, let me say that I understand that many of you men had no father in your lives. Some of you had your mother's latest live-in with the problems that brings. Others of you had it worse. You had fathers who did not delight in you. Those fathers at best, were distant and uninvolved and at worst were violent and abusive. Those men were not true fathers at all, but they marked you, their sons, with the wounds of being fatherless. I beg you to try your best to read this section with an open mind. God is a good father. Something you have not experienced. You are a son He delights in. He hungers to draw you close and bring healing to the father's wounds and scars in your life. I hope that you will find some healing and encouragement here. There is healing and wholeness for you. It is a process and a journey, but God the true Father is calling you and I to Him for true fathering.)

Always a son, often a brother, seldom a father! There! I said it! And it is highly accurate. Many Christians never move beyond the very basics of sonship, that position we refer to as being born again or saved. Unfortunately, we don't all move into the deeper things of God, including relationships with other believers, and personal evangelism for the purpose of spreading the Good News of the Kingdom of God. Because of that, we have failed many along the way. That is harsh, but it has been my experience, and I know it to be true in the lives of others as well. I believe God is calling us to be more than sons, more than brothers. He is calling us to be spiritual fathers to men around us in this, our generation. I also believe that we, His Church, have a responsibility to extend His promise of being fathers to the fatherless. *Psalms 68:5* ***Father of the fatherless*** *and protector of widows is God in his holy habitation.* (emphasis mine). With all the problems of fatherless children in our society, the Church must seek to alleviate, where possible, the negative aspect of life with no father. Fatherless children have no age limit. Seventy-year-old men who have never been fathered still crave it even if they don't understand what it is. We need to persist with the Lord to make us benevolent fathers.

Beginning with Paul's letter to the Corinthians, I will attempt to give us a working definition of fathers for the purpose of this writing. First a father is more than a guide, he is an invested teacher. Think about your Christian life. How many times in your struggle or hunger has someone given you a scripture, or told you to attend church, read the Bible, pray more, just believe, or stand on the Word. Lots of helpful sounding general direction, but no real help. Guides, but not fathers. A father is one who invests himself in my development as a son intending to help me grow into a mature man. I remember a couple of examples in my life. My dad taught me to swing a hammer when I was just five or six. He gave me an old board, a box of nails, and a hammer. He did not just say "have at it." Instead, he took my hand, wrapped it around the handle with my thumb, extended up the handle as a "guide to orient the swing," then wrapped his hand around mine and we swung the hammer together. He repeated the process until I had a rhythm and then removed his hand, but remained close. Taking my hand again from time to time, he would refine the swing until it became second nature. Later were lessons on using old bent nails, pulling nails, using the right nail for the job. Fathering. He was personally invested in this small task and it remains with me today.

Paul lived with the Corinthians for several years while establishing the church. He then kept connected through letters, sending Timothy and others to strengthen them, and visiting again. They never had to question if Paul was committed to them. He demonstrated it repeatedly in word and deed. In this same manner, we need to approach our relationships with men (our brothers) intending to create a long term commitment with them. This is particularly true with men who have not been fathered by natural fathers in their lives. Their process to this point is to figure it out through trial and error, or just say, "forget it" and walk away. This applies as well to those who have been poorly fathered or abused by their natural fathers. Much effort is required to build the relationship of trust that is required before any real fathering can occur. Trust is the foundation on which all fathering is built.

Continuing with the definition - a Father is one from whom I draw my identity. I think here of the Tolkein book *The Hobbit*. The dwarf prince, Thorin Oakenshield, is staking his claim to the Misty Mountain and the kingdom therein. He is Thorin son of Thrain son of Thror, king under the mountain. His entire identity is wrapped up in who his father and grandfather were. He points to that as his right to inherit. In our current world we have many names like Johnson, Fredrickson and Richardson. All these point back to a heritage of being the son of a father. In the Bible, Jesus refers to Peter as Simon Bar-Jonah - Simon son of Jonah. We draw our identity from our fathers, whether or not we like it. Fatherless men will themselves often abandon children to the fatherless life they suffered. One sign of being fathered is that we emulate the men who fathered us. Early in my adult life I was fists and wits against the world, in the image of my father. Later, I developed grace and mercy, the ability to remain silent when my words would not help even though I had the wisdom needed in a situation. Acting like the step-father who became Dad. My ministry pattern is a combination of several spiritual fathers. My identity is expressed through the living out of my life.

When we have been fathered, others will approach us and give credit for our father's attributes. "I know your father and he is honest to a fault, I'm sure you will be as well." My first credit account came as a result of my father. I was 16 and buying gas at the same station Dad had in his life. Dad had been gone for two years when the owner said to me, "Robert, I knew your Dad to be a good man. If you need to get gas on account here, just let me know." No credit check, no proof of employment, just "I knew your

Dad." We still do that in our culture today. We give the sons the attributes of the father. Unfortunately, it is often in the negative "the apple doesn't fall far from the tree." We do take on the attributes of our fathering or the lack thereof. As Paul writes to the Corinthians, "I urge you, then, be imitators of me." It is my hope that more of us will become like our Father so we can say with confidence, "copy my behavior."

Hebrews 12:6-8 For the Lord disciplines the one he loves, and chastises every son whom he receives." (7) It is for discipline that you have to endure. God is treating you as sons. For what son is there whom his father does not discipline? (8) If you are left without discipline, in which all have participated, then you are illegitimate children and not sons.

A true father imparts discipline to his sons. Sadly, in the American church today we have begun to create generations of "bastards" by failing to apply discipline to their lives. We excuse some sexual immorality with "well, it's just the culture we live in" and others with "they were born that way." We approve the breaking of the covenant of marriage for "incompatibility or irreconcilable differences" code words, for I'm selfish and want to have my own way. We gloss over sin in the pews and then are shocked when that same sin manifests in the pulpit. We cheat on our taxes, defraud our employers, tell lies of convenience, and when that manifests in public figures, we call for their heads. Fatherlessness pervades our society and the church, and part of that is the lack of fatherly discipline.

Discipline is a scary topic, because the line between discipline and abuse is a fine one. Abuse will always attempt to control and rule through fear, and will excuse itself by claiming to be exercising discipline. Discipline seeks to bring correction, not gain control or punish. True discipline is carried out in love and only administered in the context of a relationship. Without love, a father cannot discipline, he can only punish. Oddly, discipline often costs the father and rewards the recipient. It always hurt me to have to discipline my children. I often let things go too far before stepping in. That is bad fathering as well, because to one whose bad behavior has been ignored, discipline will feel like punishment. Let's look at some of the scriptures about discipline.

1 Thessalonians 5:14 And we urge you, brothers, admonish the idle, encourage the fainthearted, help the weak, be patient with them all.

1 Timothy 5:1-2 Do not rebuke an older man but encourage him as you would a father, younger men as brothers, (2) older women as mothers, younger women as sisters, in all purity.

1 Peter 4:8 Above all, keep loving one another earnestly, since love covers a multitude of sins.

True discipline is summed up with several words here. Admonish - "Hey that's not good." We must be bold enough to say it. Encourage - "There is a better way, this is it. You can do this." Help - Stand with, walk with, demonstrate and encourage - stand with them in prayer. Patience - patience comes with long-suffering, which means to suffer long. Discipline requires the father to suffer quietly while leading by example, with encouragement and patience. Discipline is almost always private, not public.

Calling someone out creates wounding and damages the foundation of trust. (It should be acknowledged that true discipline may be more complicated in rare cases, where one just does not respond to 'one on one' love. In that case, follow Matthew 18:15-17 which in the extreme leads to expulsion from the group. I have never had to go that far. True sons want to be pleasing to the Father.)

From beginning to end, discipline requires love to be the motivation. We have likely been guilty of the same or similar offenses. If we were disciplined properly, we will remember it, and if improperly we remember that as well. Think about your own life and recall how you were treated when you needed discipline. I remember my seasons of being corrected as valuable and saving me from a worse fate. I imagine you do as well.

Benevolent Father - invested teacher, imparter of my identity, loving disciplinarian, and finally and most important is one who has a living, loving, serving relationship with God the Father.

1 John 2:12-14 I am writing to you, little children, because your sins are forgiven for his name's sake. (13) I am writing to you, fathers, because you know him who is from the beginning. I am writing to you, young men, because you have overcome the evil one. I write to you, children, because you know the Father. (14) I write to you, fathers, because you know him who is from the beginning. I write to you, young men, because you are strong, and the word of God abides in you, and you have overcome the evil one.

This passage follows our sons, brothers, fathers' narrative. Children are aware of their forgiveness and know the father loves them. Young men go to war with evil and overcome Satan's schemes through knowledge and application of the Word of God by living it out of their hearts. But fathers, know (by experience and relationship) Jesus, who was from before time. In this knowing, they impart His heart to others by their words and action. They are men of prayer and the word, known not as monks and students, but as men of action, because they 'live' their knowledge and experience out loud for all to see the Savior. Of all the things, an outward relationship with God through Jesus is the marker to look for in fathers.

So with these explanations in mind, how do we find fathers for our lives? I would love to tell you to run down to the "We Be Fathers" store and grab one off the lot, but it is not that easy. Spiritually I was fatherless from my 17th to my 35th birthday. I wandered in the world, made my own way, and such until the need to return to the Lord became a thing. In that return, for the first time, I really set out to be more than a saved son. I wanted to know the scriptures, and I wanted to be "right." What I was looking for was law. What God was offering was 'relationship.' Slowly this picture became clear, and I started looking to my pastor. I had several pastors that failed or disappointed me in fathering, and I am sure that my actions and response failed them the same way. Perhaps my demands were too much. More likely, they were teachers and equippers, but not the father that I needed. I look back and know I learned lessons from each of them. Where I know I was wrong, I have attempted to heal the breach and hold no ill will towards any man.

It was a confusing season until I met men who just wanted to be in God's presence or hear His voice. So beginning with, I would say pray. Ask God to reveal who you should learn from in addition to your pastor. Take a hard look at the men in your circle and seek out the ones who quietly let it slip that the Lord has been speaking to them. Look at the ones who serve with humility. The ones who take an interest in how your spirit is doing. They ask questions like, what scripture have you been reading lately? What is God doing in your life? What do you feel God is saying to you? Have you sensed some type of calling? (Calling is God's chosen purpose for a man at this season of his life. It can be a tire changer or computer programmer. It does not have to be a ministry position, although it may be. Calling is a thing that brings out the passion in your being.) He may show interest in other things you are doing, but his real interest is helping you get closer to God.

This kind of man will usually not offer opinions until asked. Instead, he will solicit information and listen. He will then ask you questions that lead you to the Lord's answers. He will be well versed in scripture, but not necessarily a scholar. The scripture is lived out in his life. You will probably have to approach him. He will have a sense of who God would have him seek to father. If he extends the opportunity to fellowship, accept it. I have found that spiritual fathers usually have several sons at differing levels of development. Many of them are like me, they don't even realize they have become a father to you until they hear it from you or someone you told. They are simply content to be relational and speak into your life as God leads. If after a few attempts of connection you don't feel welcomed in, move on. Nothing is wrong with you, or them. God just has another connection for you.

This was my pattern until about ten years ago. There is another, and I think a better path. Ask God to Father you and send men to enhance that fathering. What I found was He would send men to me. They sought me out. Invited me into fellowship. Drew me into conversation. Shared their experience and insight with me. When asked, they would comment on what they were asked, but never sought to take over, just offered wisdom and advice. They wanted to know how to pray for me and opened doors here and there. That's what fathers do. They are concerned about the success of sons. Notice that I said they. Different men have fathered me in different areas of my life, and that is the way it will likely be for you. My advice. Move significantly into the position of bonded brother and ask God to Father you. Then wait. It will come and with it, wisdom and fellowship that is priceless.

But what about becoming a father? I have some news for you, you already are. I call it unintentional fathering. Men you know are looking at you and making their decisions to follow God like you lead, or maybe deciding to reject Him all together. Your day-to-day life preaches a sermon without words and men read that sermon and make life decisions. As an example, I will take my grandson. He was one-year-old when he came to live with me. We are not blood related, nor do we look alike. But I have fathered him, intentionally, with kindness and love and discipline, engaging in teachable moments, and drawing him into a father - son relationship. When he was about five, he asked if I would be his Daddy. I had been Papa for the previous four years. Today he is 21 and heading out on his own. It is not all either of us would have hoped. Some of the intentional lessons he rejects, but it is his journey. It is my job to remain Dad. The fun thing is in the unintentional fathering. He stands like I do. Talks with his hands. Uses the same turns of phrase. Finds interest in eating new things. He is a good young man and I am proud of him. The point is, he took on many of the things I taught, and rejected others. But the things I modeled unconsciously, those he has incorporated into his life.

That is the bulk of what fathering really is. If you would be a good father, be a good model. You won't be perfect. None of us are. Teaching is good, relationships are better. As Paul challenged in our beginning scripture, "be imitators of me." I would change that up and say be worthy of imitation. Model humility. Apologize when you are wrong. Avoid saying "I told you so" instead say "where do you think we go from here?" Our goal is not to have perfect sons, but to have sons that seek the perfection of God's maturity. We are already fathering, let's let Paul's admonition to Timothy be our guide.

2 Timothy 2:1-2 You then, my child, be strengthened by the grace that is in Christ Jesus, (2) and what you have heard from me in the presence of many witnesses entrust to faithful men who will be able to teach others also.

So what about intentional fathering and where do the faithful men come from? We don't just get up one morning and decide we are going to be spiritual fathers. It is part of our journey as followers of the Christ. My advice is to surround yourself with brothers. Seek and submit to fathering. Pray, "Lord, make me a good father in your image." And watch what happens. Again, there will be those who seek you out. It usually starts small with a question about life, or sharing of a life story, or "asking for a friend - wink wink." A listening ear with thoughtful response will plant the seeds for future conversations. One of my habits is to walk with men outside, by the river, in the foothills, down a country road or just up and down the sidewalk. Something about walking and outdoors tears down walls and promotes conversation. If someone wants to get a coffee, do that. Don't just jump into the stuff. Being open is tough on guys. It may take two or three coffee shop visits talking about ball games, fishing and whatever the issue is not, just for them to decide you are worthy of sharing this information with you. Patience, care, encouragement, and prayer are the tools God gives you. His Holy Spirit will also download information into your conversations in a timely and effective manner. Be open to respond with the little nudges that pass through your mind as you chew the second doughnut. The Spirit's timing is perfect.

There will also be those you need to go after for fathering. For me, it works like this. I think of someone unexpectedly, maybe a dream, or they pop into my head. I begin with prayer for them right then before I forget. I ask God to bless them and care for them at that moment. I ask if there is something He would like me to communicate, or am I just to pray and wait? It happens both ways. If they are part of my group already, I may wait until a men's meeting, or church service and pull them aside with the "I was thinking about you this week and prayed for God's blessing on your life" opening. Then I ask how they are and let them talk. It is amazing to me the number of times God has me pray exactly when someone is going through something.

On the strength of that prayer, the answer comes to the person I am praying for, with no other involvement required. If the person is not someone I see normally, I send them a text or a call with the same, "I'm praying for you" information. I will then ask if they would like to get together. Many new relationships start this way. You will have to find your own rhythm with this.

There is the goal, committing what you have learned to another generation. **Fathering!** I challenge you to continue to grow as a son. Be sharpened and resharpened by your brothers. And raise sons to be fathers. You have what it takes.

I want to close this chapter with the delicate discussion about fathering ladies. Ladies need fathers too! It is a tricky situation and can be a slippery slope to disaster. Every lady needs to gain the understanding that they are lovely and worth pursuing. They also need to know not to give in to the yahoo's who would simply use them and discard them. Many of them have already experienced the yahoo's and now need to know that God will make all things new in their lives. I have two rules about fathering ladies. One is the Mother, Sister, Daughter Rule. Never say or do anything to or with a lady that you would not desire that a completely strange man would do to your mother, sister, or daughter. That rule is the one that keeps your name out of the paper and away from lawsuits. My second rule is No Private Contact with any woman, not my wife or natural daughter. Period. No secret phone calls, text messages, private meetings. Bring your wife. Turn on the speaker phone. Change the text to a group text with your wife included. If you are not married, try to shift the load to a mature couple, or engage the help of a mature female leader from the church, It is never okay to violate these two rules. Seek to be the 'dad' they need you to be by protecting them and yourself.

Questions for Reflection

1. Do you have a desire to be fathered? It begins here. We all need it desperately. If the answer is no I implore you to seek the Lord in prayer and follow His leading. He will place trustworthy fathers in your life.

2. Are you connected to a circle of men with whom you have close fellowship? If not, please start to seek one out. This circle may be unique to you with three or four guys from different arenas and not connected to each other. You and I need our circles.

3. Are you being Fathered now? If not, begin to pursue fathers for your life. There is a great freedom and healing in finding God's fathers for you.

4. Are you seeking to be intentional in your fathering? Remember you are fathering by your example. Be intentional about it.

Note: If this chapter has provoked a desire to know more about healing the father wounds in your heart. I would recommend the book ***Fathered By God***, by John Eldredge as the next step on your journey.

Chapter 7

The Journey Continues

Genesis 5:22-24 Enoch walked with God after he fathered Methuselah 300 years and had other sons and daughters. (23) Thus all the days of Enoch were 365 years. (24) Enoch walked with God, and he was not, for God took him.

I love this thought. Enoch walked with God, after the fall, before the flood. No salvation, no Bible, no church attendance, just a one-on-one talk and walk with God. And as he does, one day God says, "enough, come home with me." Most of us would love to have that happen. Few of us have the determination to walk 300 minutes, much less 300 years. As I have alluded to in previous chapters, this life is a journey. It is full of challenges and pitfalls as well as great looking side roads that lead to traps. Then there are the narrow, seemingly impassable trails that lead to great treasures. And what about the long stretches of road with seemingly no end, just the mindless repetition of another day? Avoiding the traps, choosing the challenging terrain and surviving the mundane, that I lay before you, this last chapter. We are on a journey. All of us. Headed to the end of this life and the beginning of the next. Every day we

have is a gift from God and He has a great purpose for it.
Our part is to find that purpose and live it.

*Jeremiah 6:16 Thus says the LORD: "Stand by the roads,
and look, and ask for the ancient paths, where the good
way is; and walk in it, and find rest for your souls. But they
said, 'We will not walk in it.'"*

This is a sad passage in a way. The Lord says He
will show us where to walk and we will find rest but they,
and too many of us, say no. We will not. This is the
beginning point, though. God calls and says follow, and we
have to decide. If you read the Bible, from Abraham's call
to go to an unknown place that God would show him, to
Jesus calling the disciples to follow Him and become
fishers of men, you find journey after journey. In fact, a
large portion of the scripture is simply the telling of the
stories of ordinary men, finding an extraordinary life by
submitting to the leading of a perfect Creator. The most
exciting thing about this truth is He is still calling ordinary
men to extraordinary lives. We just need to ask where the
road is and then walk in it!

Many would say, "but I do ask and God never says
anything." I used to feel that way too. Consider this. God
promised each person to always be there and to never leave
us alone. Jesus repeated the promise. If those promises
aren't trustworthy, then the whole thing is a lie. So if we
believe the Scripture, if we have trusted Jesus for our
salvation, then we must believe the promises are true. What
I have had to learn is, what God's voice sounds like? Well,
that's easy. Except when it's not. Sometimes He speaks
through Scripture. So I must read and commit to memory.

Sometimes through song, so I need to worship. Sometimes through sermons, so I must attend services. But He also speaks to us inside. It sounds like our own thoughts, our own voice, and it is spoken in words we understand. Sometimes His voice to me is "what were you thinking knot-head…you know better?" Can you believe God would talk that way. He does to me because I can hear it. God speaks to us individually in a way we can hear. If we are convinced we can't hear personally, He will speak through friends and neighbors, pastors and Scripture, whatever He must do to get us to hear the message. He is speaking to you even now. One way He speaks to me is through what I call Divine Impulse. I get the impulse to do something in a different way, out of the ordinary, take the long way home kind of leading. I may feel that I should turn down this way, or call this person. That is the impulse. After years I have learned to usually recognize when it is His voice and when I should not have had that extra slice of pizza. You have had those impulses too. Try following them like this. Pray that God would speak to you through impulse for the next week. Then follow out of each impulse, see where it leads. It will sharpen your hearing. God won't lead you into sin, to violate the speed limit, cheat on your wife, or beat up the mayor even though he deserves it. God will lead you into things for His purpose and then use you to accomplish it.

The way is not always clear! A couple of years ago we took a western road trip to see Mt. Rushmore and other things in the area. We decided to travel through the Badlands National Park. It was gorgeous and mysterious, but the roads were well marked and the day beautiful so we continued. As it began to get later in the day, we looked at the map and saw that one of the National Park's roads exited the park onto a state road that led into the town where we were heading for the night. So, we continued down this road because it was a good 60 miles shorter than going out the main entrance and by interstate. It was great, we saw buffalo and antelope, grouse and numerous other small animals, and then it wasn't great. The road turned to dirt. No warning. No end to the park. No signs. No GPS, just my Rand McNally Atlas (Yes I am of that generation). Well, it said the road connected, but that was the only clue. We decided to trust and keep going. After 30 miles of dirt road, we found pavement and a sign. Three unmarked country roads later, we popped out within a mile of our hotel. So it is on the journey with God. His word, or some other leading like *Isaiah 30:21 And your ears shall hear a word behind you, saying, "This is the way, walk in it," when you turn to the right or when you turn to the left.* Like we were with the Atlas, we trusted the map makers had been there and knew the way. God has been ahead of you and laid out the way. Sometimes it is a great distance between markers and the GPS seems to be out, but He is there. Keep going in faith and He will see you to your destination.

But what if I blow it? Well, you are in good company. Abraham twice lied about Sarah being his wife and she was taken into harems twice. He also tried to make prophecy come true with Sarah's maid which resulted in Ishmael the father of all Arab nations. We are still paying for that one and yet Abraham is called the "Father of the Faithful." David, took a friend's wife and had the friend murdered to cover it up, and yet he is called "Friend of God." Peter was the leader of the Disciples and denied knowing Jesus three times during the crucifixion trial. Three

Times Peter!!! Really!!!! Fifty odd days later, the Holy Spirit comes and the same Peter preaches the first sermon with 3000 people responding to the message of salvation. Your struggles have nothing on these guys. My favorite one and personal hero is Jonah. God says go here. Jonah says, "no I will not." And winds up in the belly of a great fish. After three days Nineveh sounds pretty good so Jonah says "I'm sorry." So there in Chapter 3, we find Jonah laying on the beach, covered in fish puke and seaweed, skin bleaching out half digested and stinking to high heaven. And the Word of the Lord came to Jonah a second time. "Are you ready yet? I need you to go to Nineveh!" So if God would still choose Jonah, I know He has a use for you and me.

Sometimes I thought I had missed God's plan because problems filled my life, or temptations kept coming. I just had to keep moving. God said to follow where He would lead and He would show us, keep us, guide us, and protect us. Some days my life doesn't feel like I am being protected. I'm sure you know the feeling, but we are being watched over and cared for more than we can imagine. Consider the following passages.

1 Peter 4:12 Beloved, do not be surprised at the fiery trial when it comes upon you to test you, as though something strange were happening to you.

It is not strange to be tested. We should not be surprised. When we make the decision to follow Jesus and embrace His teachings and lifestyle, we make an enemy of Satan and a good portion of the world (Unfortunately this can include a large number of friends and family which is why we need the brotherhood!) He warned that we would be rejected and troubled in many different ways (which is contrary to the American idea that it should be all peaches and cream all the time). Reading through Acts we find some believers persecuted, beaten, stoned, executed and driven out. Others were imprisoned or had to run away to other towns. Their response? They went everywhere preaching the Good News of the Kingdom. We should do the same. I think it drives my enemies crazy when I don't let trials overwhelm me. (Yes I feel them and hate them just as much as you do. I am just not going to agonize over it. Instead I will pray and do my best. Deliverance will come.)

1 Corinthians 10:13 (13) No temptation has overtaken you that is not common to man. God is faithful, and he will not let you be tempted beyond your ability, but with the temptation he will also provide the way of escape, that you may be able to endure it.

Here is the heart of the matter. I have learned to stop praying the "take it away" prayer. Those usually don't work, or if it does, it is only temporary and will come back again shortly. When the trials and temptations come, I have found them to be formative for my life. He strengthens me so that I can go through it, not escape from it. It is in the fire of going through that I am refined. That refining disarms my enemy and I come out more like Jesus than when I went in. This pattern has repeated itself in my life for years. Trial comes. I quit whining and start enduring. And yes, I pray. I pray the "what do you want me to learn, what are you showing men, what are you doing in my life here" prayers. He in turn leads me through. The enemy loses and I grow from the experience. This is the Journey! Spreading the Kingdom and becoming more like Jesus.

2 Corinthians 2:14 But thanks be to God, who in Christ always leads us in triumphal procession, and through us spreads the fragrance of the knowledge of him everywhere.

This is the promise that is true beyond all the enemy's challenges. He promises to lead me if I stay centered in to who Jesus is and continue to trust Him even in the most impossible of circumstances. The list of times He has brought me through is long and still growing. I am sure it is the same for you. Every time we grow in Him, it spreads the aroma of the Kingdom. Like the Robert Duvall line from *Apocalypse Now.* "I love the smell of Napalm in the morning....it smells like… victory." When we follow the Lord through trials, we come out covered in His fragrance and it smells like VICTORY! Others notice and witness goes forward and the Kingdom advances. Journey! I could go on and on, but you get the message. We follow and He leads as some old time preachers say, "from victory to victory, from faith to faith, and from glory to glory." I used to think that was a verse, instead it is a compilation of several verses and principles that piece together and demonstrate the believer's journey. The other side of this sentence we need to understand is this. When we move from victory to victory, we have moved from battle to battle. Battle first, then victory. When we move from faith to faith, we are required to believe beyond where we believed before. My 8-year-old Sunday School faith is not sufficient to pray when I need to see God move in power in my life. When we move from glory to glory, it means that we have endured the refining trials in His presence and now we look more like Him.

I want to leave you with three things for your journey that have helped me. There are many, but these three are significant. I hope they will benefit you as your journey continues.

Philippians 2:12-13 Therefore, my beloved, as you have always obeyed, so now, not only as in my presence but much more in my absence, work out your own salvation with fear and trembling, (13) for it is God who works in you, both to will and to work for his good pleasure.

Seek to be obedient. Connect to a body of believers. Understand that we do not do this in our own strength. Temptations and trials come. The world is condemned already. All we can do is follow the Master. If you seek that, He will change you from the inside.

Micah 7:8 Rejoice not over me, O my enemy; when I fall, I shall rise; when I sit in darkness, the LORD will be a light to me.

You will fail. We all do. The thing is, when you find yourself in the "poop," don't roll around in it or build an altar to grief and failure. Get up, wash up. Cry out to the Lord. "Lord, it's me... again... with this... again... lead me out." He will be faithful to rescue you.

2 Timothy 1:6-7 For this reason I remind you to fan into flame the gift of God, which is in you through the laying on of my hands, (7) for God gave us a spirit not of fear but of power and love and self-control.

Fan the flame of His Spirit within yourself. Study and memorize Scripture. Think about it some every day.

Don't be afraid. It is His mission we are on. All the power we need, all the love required, all the self-control is provided. We simply must follow and obey.

Lastly, remember this. Every man's journey is as individual and personal as His relationship with God. We will all have some things in common, but there are places men have to go alone with the Lord and we can only encourage them to go and wait for their return. Don't try to force yourself or anyone else into a one size fits all mold. It is a personal relationship. Walk it out and encourage others in theirs.

I want to thank you for taking time to read this. I hope I have challenged you to connect with the Lord and with fellow believers in a new and deeper way. If you have never had a relationship with the Lord, look at Appendix A and check out what He has promised for you. You have a testimony, a story, even if you have never shared it. Check Appendix B for a way to develop your own testimony. God bless and keep you my fellow Prodigals. Hope to see you on His road. Bob

Questions for Reflection

1. Have I decided for myself that life is a journey? Why or why not?

2. Have I stopped at some place along the way like it is a destination (salvation, church membership, sonship)? If so, what do I need to do to get moving with Him again?

3. Do I continue to follow His last directions even when the way ahead is unclear?

4. Am I providing encouragement and help to those who are on their journey?

Appendix A: Joining the Journey

Romans 5:8, but God shows his love for us in that while we were still sinners, Christ died for us.

In spite of our behavior and attitude, God loves us anyway. He desires us to be connected. We are unable to do right all the time, so God made for us a way of escape to return to Him.

Romans 6:23, For the wages of sin is death, but the free gift of God is eternal life in Christ Jesus our Lord.

Now we will all die a natural death. Some by accident, some by crime, some by old age, but all die. This verse, however, refers to the death of eternity, the eternal separation from God. There are many bad things that go with the second death, but I have good news. Jesus, the Christ (Savior), came to Earth as man, lived a sinless life and died on the cross to pay the debt of our sin. He died in our place so we may avoid the second death, but something is required of us.

Romans 10:9-10, because, if you confess with your mouth that Jesus is Lord and believe in your heart that God raised him from the dead, you will be saved. (10) For with the heart one believes and is justified, and with the mouth one confesses and is saved.

This is what is required. Believe, not just with my mind, but in the core of my being, we say from the heart. To be convinced without a shadow of a doubt. If I was trying to throw you out of an airplane at 10,000 feet with no parachute, would you believe I was trying to kill you? Without a shadow of a doubt you would, and you would resist with all that is within you, to resist being thrown from the plane. We have earned death, but God wants for us to believe and be saved. So what will you do? It is your choice. He loves you, makes a way for you, begs you to come, but He will not make you. Your love for Him must be freely given. You and you alone can decide. If you sense within yourself that, "Yes! I want this!" This is what to do next.

You need to ask in prayer. Prayer is just a conversation with God. I would suggest something like this, but the words are not as important as your sincere heart when you pray. You can pray alone or with another believer.

"Father God, I have come to understand that I have sinned by not following your plan for my life. I want that to change. I accept that your son Jesus died for me and paid for my sin so I do not have to. I believe in the work that He did on the cross and ask that You receive me according to the promise of Your word. I believe and accept it is done and will follow You now as an adopted son on the rest of my journey."

Once you have done this, there are some next steps. If you know a brother that is a believer, call and tell him, in your own words, what you have done. This is called giving a testimony - a story of what God has done in your life. You are now saved. Your future with God is secure, but your journey is still ahead. You will need to find a body of believers where you fit. They will be your tribe. You will need to be baptized in water. This is your public declaration. You also need to connect with brothers who will walk with you on your journey.

Welcome to the family brother. My prayer for you is you find the fullness of all God has for you and that you embrace it fully. God bless you on your journey. Your Brother, Bob Grant.

Appendix B:
Telling Your Story

Revelation 12:11, And they have conquered him by the blood of the Lamb and by the word of their testimony, for they loved not their lives even unto death.

If you arrived here and have wondered what is this all about, really? Then I want to spend a few lines breaking it down for you. Me, you, and everyone else we know was born, through no fault of our own, with a rebellious nature. We are self-centered and greedy and want everything our own way. That happened thousands of years ago when Adam and Eve, the first people, used their gift of free will and chose to violate God's rules and do things their own way. As a result, they received the curse of violating God's rules, and their descendants (all of mankind) are born under a curse of separation from God. All of us. Even the most beautiful, precious, tiny infant is born into that curse.

The Good News is that we don't have to stay there. God has always had a plan to restore us to Himself. His plan requires our cooperation. Think of it this way. As an American, when I reach the age of 18, I have the right to vote. But I can't just vote any way or any time or any place I choose. I have to register and verifying my address. I have to vote at a certain polling station or obtain an official absentee ballot. I have to vote during the prescribed time for voting. I can't write my vote on a truck stop napkin and mail it in to Congress and expect it to be counted. So if I don't follow the rules, though voting is my right, my vote doesn't count.

In the same manner, all of us have the right to become the sons of God. But there is a pattern we must follow to gain access to that right. Here are some things to think about.

Romans 3:23, for all have sinned and fall short of the glory of God.

All of us have missed the mark. Sin is simply that which is contrary to God's will for us. It is not just the behavior (lie, cheat, steal), but the attitude of the heart that says these things are okay. If you ever lied, you sinned. Simple, accept it and look to the next line.

This passage comes from John's vision of Heaven when he was on the Island of Patmos in exile for having preached the Gospel of Jesus everywhere he went. He records seeing a great multitude of ascended believers at the trial of Satan. This is their record. They overcame Satan by the Blood and by their testimony, and they had died to themselves. It is our testimony that I am focusing on here.

Testimony is simply the telling of my story or experience. In a court, a person's testimony is revealing what they know about the events before the court. Eyewitness testimony is considered being of the greatest importance when hearing a case. It is very valuable. In the same manner, our testimony (story) of what God has done for and in our lives is incredibly valuable in sharing the Good News with others. In the day we now live, many people do not believe in God or in the Bible and are not particularly interested in what the Bible says. There are many reasons for this beyond this discussion. I just ask that you accept it for now. What makes our testimony so valuable is they cannot refute it. When I say this is what happened to me, they have to hear it as truth. Their opinion doesn't matter; it is my testimony. We must all be able to tell our own story. I am going to give you some patterns to look at and adapt to your own story. I think you should write your story out and spend time memorizing it so you can tell it quickly and confidently without hesitation. You should also be able to answer questions about what brought you to those events and what you felt like after. I would suggest you have multiple testimonies based on which life event you need to share. I put them in two categories, salvation, and events after salvation. I will list some of my own. You can use them as a pattern using your actual experiences.

My salvation story. "When I was about 12 years old, I had been attending a local church with friends. I attended Sunday School and such, not because of faith, but it was an accepted social activity in the 1960s America. You got to see your friends and usually had some Kool-Aid and snacks of some kind. That morning I stayed for the Sunday morning service. I don't remember what songs were sung or what the pastor preached on, but I do remember, what is called the invitation, at the end of the service. In an invitation, people in the service are given an opportunity to respond to the message of the Good News. Namely, I have been a sinner and am apart from God and I need Him to save me. I had heard the invitation multiple times, but this Sunday something was different. All of a sudden I seemed to realize that I was responsible for my own decision and I needed to be saved. My feet were in the aisle and my hands were gripping the back of the pew until I finally turned loose and went forward. I was weeping over my sin and emotionally distraught. The pastor led me through a prayer, and at the end of that I felt like the weight of the world had lifted off of me. I was relieved. My sin had been forgiven, and I was saved." After you have shared a story like this, you can add, "God wants to do this for you as well." You should be able to answer some questions others may have about the experience.

Baptism Testimony. "I remember being excited for baptism. Everyone in my family was there. There were several of us being baptized. We put on white cotton robes and walked into the tank. The pastor put each of us under the water with the words "I baptize you in the name of the Father, and the Son, and the Holy Spirit" and then he lifted us back up. I felt clean. Some people felt heat, but I just felt clean and at peace. Again, your story will likely be different, but it is important to tell it.

Return Testimony: "I left Church when I went off to college at 17. I was disillusioned about the death of my Father and not understanding why God would take him (He didn't). It would be 18 years later when I would be sick of myself and my life, and said one day out loud, 'if I don't get back in Church, I'm not going to make it.' That is when I started looking to be engaged with God again. After prayer and searching, I found a local congregation and began to learn that true Church life was about relationships, not just doing good deeds, or choosing the right thing. I learned that I could pray, hear God's voice in my inner self. I found that scripture made more sense and wondered why I ever left. I had found my way back to the path and once again I was at peace." This is my story, and there are enough of these to write a book. In fact, I might call it "Been There Done That - Got the Marks."

We all have stories of how God has helped us in impossible circumstances. I can testify about finances, call to ministry, marriage restoration, children restored to the family, miraculous healing and crazy adventures where no explanation suffices except God did this for me. You have your own set. Write them down. Commit them to memory and share them whenever it is appropriate to do so. Testimony is the most powerful witness for the Kingdom I have found. It provokes people to ask and investigate faith. We need to tell and they need to hear. God Bless.

Bob Grant brings a conversational ministry style which
may include healing and prophecy as the Holy Spirit leads.
An equipper: he endeavors to impart ministry knowledge
and experience into his hearers. Messages are challenging
and instructive, pointing the faithful to the next steps on
their journey. His strong planning and
organizational background helps create foundations for
aggressive Church ministry. His passion is to equip the
small Church and especially the men of the small Church
for the spiritual battles we are engaged in today.

Bob is available for seminars, conferences and individual
meetings. He is also available for consultation.

He may be contacted at:

pastorbob14011@gmail.com
or
Bob Grant, P.O. Box 66, Kill Buck, NY 14748